Jim Clark
Grand Prix Legend

For my wife Ruby

Jim Clark
Grand Prix Legend
Andrew Tulloch

WEIDENFELD & NICOLSON

Contents

Foreword
by Sir Stirling Moss

IN A RECENT BOOK I SEE that I was placed number one in a listing of the best Formula 1 drivers of all time 'separated by a thin margin' from Jimmy Clark at number two. Jimmy and I only overlapped for about a year and a half at the very start of his FI career and before mine was ended by my shunt. So we never competed for any length of time, but I was aware of this precocious new talent emerging. I guess it was the Monaco Grand Prix in 1961 – one of my best ever races – that I noticed him properly for the first time as a new boy, though amongst the new generation the one that first caught my eye was Innes Ireland. Innes was a bit of a hell raiser, but on his day he was as quick as anyone and when he first came to Goodwood he beat me in two races in the new Lotus. Mind you, Colin Chapman would never sell Rob Walker, my patron, the latest Lotus. We had to wait a year so I was always racing against the latest model. Innes was eventually fired from Lotus in favour of Jimmy so I suppose that tells you something about Colin Chapman's estimate of their relative merits. We also raced at different venues: Jimmy would go with Lotus to Pau, a nice non-championship course in the South of France, early in the year, and that always clashed with a Goodwood meet which I used to go to as it was closer to home if anything went wrong with the car.

I helped found the Grand Prix Drivers Association with Graham Hill in 1961, as a sort of drivers union. We used to have regular meetings to talk

about things like public safety or the deployment of marshals or fire-proof overalls or whether the driver on pole could choose the left or right position on the front row and I began to get to know Jimmy better then. There is a good photograph of an impromptu GPDA meeting we both attended on pages 58–59 of this book. I don't think we ever talked about driver safety much. None of us ever wore seat belts – so that you could escape more quickly if the car caught fire, which they did frequently in those days. We all had the attitude that death and injury were part and parcel of extreme sports, and that if you felt it was too dangerous you didn't have to take part. We didn't try to slow down good circuits by introducing chicanes, but we were very keen on crowd safety. After the drivers' death-toll rose unacceptably Graham Hill and Jo Bonnier and later Jackie Stewart took up the cudgels of driver safety and the sport is now very, very different as a result. Poor Jimmy drove the most fragile, vulnerable car of all – Colin Chapman was notorious for making every component of the Lotus as light as possible, as a result of which they

The Lombank Trophy at Snetterton (though I see I have marked it 'Goodwood') on 14 April 1962, my second last race. I am on pole, with Jimmy beside me and then Graham Hill and John Surtees closest to the camera. I set the fastest lap but had trouble and came 7th. Jimmy won, a minute ahead of Graham Hill.

were constantly suffering from mechanical failure. At high speed that could be pretty dangerous.

As a group we stuck together and about eighteen to twenty of us were quite close (all the ushers at my first wedding were racing drivers) and towards the end of my career that bunch included Jimmy. I would say were friends, but not pals. The bunch of us used to do things like shop together and if we were buying shoes ask the shopkeeper for a bulk discount! I found Jimmy (we all called him Jimmy although the public seemed to prefer Jim) a quite private person, a bit of an introvert. If we were all larking about or talking about girls he didn't really join in. On the other hand he was very friendly, not at all dour and quick to laugh. He was also quite humble, he appeared to be unaware of how good he really was and never traded on his growing fame. He found the perfect racing partner in Colin Chapman. Jimmy was a smooth, balanced driver who had a great understanding of what he could do with a car, and Colin was a technical genius who would make it work for him. Every car was set up for an individual driver – if I drove a car set up for Jack Brabham and vice versa we wouldn't have been nearly so quick.

In 1963, after I had retired, I went out to watch the Indianapolis 500. Jim came second, though there appeared to have been a bit of rule bending about an oil leak, which denied him first place. It was very apparent then how quick he was. I would love to have raced Jim in his prime. Then we could have really contested that 1–2 place in the roll call of best F1 drivers . . .

Stirling Moss

Acknowledgements

As someone who began to watch motor racing in the later 1960s, writing this book has been an absolute pleasure, giving me an opportunity to meet people who knew Jim Clark and worked in probably the most exciting era of motor sport. In particular I would like to thank Jim's sister Betty Peddie who not only kindly spoke to me but also took time to read over the first draft of my manuscript. Likewise Ian Scott Watson has been very helpful during the preparation of this book.

I would also like to thank George and Sheila Campbell, Bob and Mary Dance for their time and hospitality. Cedric Selser and Sir John Whitmore also took time out from their busy days to speak to me. Equally Eric Bryce has given freely of his time, not just during the creation of this book but throughout the time I have been working in the Jim Clark Room.

I am grateful to Weidenfeld & Nicolson for giving me the opportunity to write this book. In particular I must thank Michael Dover, Suzanne Arnold, designer Jean-Michel Dentand, David Rowley and their other staff for their guidance and help. Additionally my employers at Scottish Borders Council have been supportive during this period. In this regard I must thank Alan Hasson, Ian Brown and Fiona Colton for allowing me to write the book. Furthermore my line manager Shona Sinclair, Curator of Hawick Museum, Rosy Hayward, the Museum & Gallery Assistant in Duns and all of the staff of Berwickshire Museums have encouraged me while I have been writing the book.

Finally I must also thank my wife Ruby who has at times seen me virtually vanish from sight while I have been working on the book. Her commonsense and support have been invaluable.

While gratefully acknowledging the help that the above people have given the final content and form of this book are my sole responsibility, as are mistakes or omissions within it.

Andrew Tulloch

Chapter 1
Background & Early Career in Scotland

JIM CLARK – ALWAYS KNOWN AS 'Jimmy' to his fellow racing drivers but 'Jim' to his family – came from farming stock that had settled in the Borders of southern Scotland. His family roots lay farther north, in Perthshire, Kinross-shire and Fife, deep in the heartlands of the old Celtic Kingdom of the Scots.

Jim's father James married Helen Niven, who was also from a farming family. They moved from Kinross-shire to Kilmany in Fife, a village close to the southern banks of the River Tay. James and Helen Clark had five children: four girls between 1925 and 1932 – Mattie, Susan, Isobel and Betty – and then, three and a half years later, on 4 March 1936, Jim was born. In the patriarchal world of the 1930s this was a big event. All Scottish families wanted a son and heir to carry on both the family name and the family business – or farm.

In 1942, six years after Jim was born, James bought a farm of some 1,400 acres in Berwickshire. It was split over two locations: one site was at Edington Mains and the other close by at Edington Hill. It was a mixed economy farm: as well as growing crops the family bred three types of sheep and imported cattle from Ireland and, for a short period, they also owned Edington Mill. The farmhouse at Edington Hill was not needed as a family home so it was divided to provide accommodation for the farm workers. And during the Second World War the arable land was increased by about 100 acres by reclaiming heath and scrubland as a

Opposite: Jim on the farm in Berwickshire. Although motor racing was his passion he was probably never more comfortable than when working on his farm.

contribution towards the government's Dig for Victory campaign, which encouraged people to keep allotments to ensure that Britain had enough food no matter how long the war lasted.

Farming then was still very much rooted in the past and although mechanisation had been increasing since the Industrial Revolution the routines of farm life would have been familiar to farmers of the eighteenth and nineteenth centuries. Tractors had begun to appear, but because of wartime fuel shortages farms reverted once more to horse-drawn power. At Edington Mains there was roughly one pair of horses for every 100 acres. One of Jim's sisters recalls that there was always an air of ritual about the farm at the start of the day. There was a strict pecking order as the ploughmen left the yard in the morning, with the steward (or farm manager) leading his horses out first.

Bill Campbell was the farm steward at Edington Mains and when James Clark purchased the farm Bill stayed on. When, later, Jim was to become more and more active in motor racing, Bill's role would be crucial.

Farms all over Britain at this time were thriving little communities. There were upwards of twenty children living around the farm at Edington, providing plenty of playmates for the Clark children. They all

Jim was always very keen on going as fast as possible. He and Alec, at a very early age, liked to attach cardboard fins to their bicycles and race around the farm buildings. They also raced around Jim's mother's garden, which was a ready-made racetrack. Helen Clark was not amused by the resulting mess.

travelled together to the local school in Chirnside, getting on the school bus at the end of the road.

Jim was an active, sporty and not very academic child, mischievous and always ready for a bit of adventure. One of his sisters remembers that one day Jim and George, one of the sons of Bill Campbell, played truant from school. Their bid for freedom lasted all of ten minutes. They had hidden in an old house when the school bus went by but they came out too soon and while wandering along the road they were rounded up and despatched to school by Jim's father.

Jim was always very keen on going as fast a possible. He and Alec, George's younger brother, at a very early age liked to attach cardboard fins to their bicycles and then race around the farm buildings. They also raced around Jim's mother's garden, which was a ready-made racetrack, laid out in squares and particularly treacherous after rain. Helen Clark was not amused by the resulting mess.

Being very sporty, Jim was also a good games player with fast reflexes. A craze for ping pong with his sister Betty, for instance, was later replaced by tennis and cricket. He played hockey at school and then for Berwick. When he was a bit older, he went shooting with his father, whereupon he demonstrated that he was also an excellent shot.

Like many farmers' children, Jim was driving vehicles around the farm long before he was of legal age to drive on public roads. During the war the family Alvis car was put on blocks and when, at the end of the war, it was recommissioned, Jim was very keen to be the one to bring it around to the door for his father to drive. After all, the Edington driveway was a good half mile from the main road between Duns and Berwick and there were many small farm tracks on which to practise his driving. Opportunities such as this were too good to be missed.

Edington Mains farm in the 1960s. In those days farms were more labour intensive and the farm was the centre of a small community.

Jim signing autographs for pupils on the bonnet of his Lotus Elan while visiting his former school, Loretto, in Musselburgh.

As the only son of a farmer, Jim's education – formal and informal – was typical of the time: he spent three years at the local primary school followed by another three years at Clifton Hall preparatory school, housed in a castellated building of baronial proportions outside Edinburgh, and finally at Loretto, Scotland's first independent boarding school, from 1946 until 1951, when he was fifteen. As the farmer's son, Jim was expected to help, particularly at harvest time and during the 'tattie holidays', when Scottish children in rural areas were given time off school, once they were twelve years old, to pick potatoes. When he was away at boarding school, though, he was spared this back-breaking task.

In 1937, Jim's grandfather had purchased a Buick, which had a radio that his grandchildren found magical. Sitting in a car and listening to people talk and play music was somehow a bit more extraordinary than listening to the radio at home. Furthermore, Jim's brother-in-law, Alec Calder, was a keen amateur racing driver and had a 3-litre Bentley that he raced at Winfield.

Perhaps details such as these helped to spark Jim's interest in racing. Another trigger lay in the fact that Jim's uncle in Kent lived near Brands Hatch and was practically in the car business. On holiday with a cousin, Jim went to the circuit and saw Stirling Moss drive. It is said that Jim asked Stirling for his autograph but it seems unlikely that he would ever have done that. As a boy – and indeed as a man – Jim was innately shy and he was always unwilling to push himself into the limelight. According to one of his sisters it is much more likely that it was their cousin who asked for the autograph on Jim's behalf. This holiday and the proximity of the two tracks in Berwickshire at Winfield and Charterhall must have played their parts in getting Jim interested in motor racing.

At some point in Jim's youth, he managed to acquire tickets for a race meeting at Charterhall. George Campbell remembers that there was a big international meeting and that Jim was keen to go and got him a ticket too. George recalls that he was definitely less enthused about this sport than Jim was; he probably got more out of the bicycle ride to get to Charterhall.

Most of the Berwick and District Motor Club's members were young farmers. Many of the competitions they entered were fairly rough and ready, completely different from the high-level events in which Jim was to make his name. Nevertheless, races such as these were essential for any aspiring young driver to hone his skills and race craft if he were to develop into a serious racing driver.

Jim's grandfather died in October 1951 and then, ten days later, his uncle, his father's youngest brother, also died. Suddenly Jim's father was left with 3,000 acres and three farms to manage and a twenty-six mile journey between his farm at Edington and the farms at Over Roxburgh and Kerchesters. This was too much for him manage alone and Jim was called home from Loretto to help out.

Jim came back to Berwickshire and took over responsibility for managing Edington Mains under the supervision of Bill Campbell. His father moved out and went to live at Kerchesters, to the south of Kelso, to manage that farm – which he ran for a year – and then the one at Over Roxburgh. Jim lived in the family home at Edington Mains with his sister Isobel installed as housekeeper. In reality, of course, Bill was actually

Jim with his mother Helen Clark and sister Betty outside Buckingham Palace in 1964 after he received his OBE.

in charge because Jim was not yet sixteen. It was a good arrangement, enabling Jim to learn from Bill how to be a farmer.

As soon as he could, after his seventeenth birthday, Jim obtained his driving licence. This allowed him to travel farther under his own steam and to develop more of a social life beyond the farm. Soon afterwards, he met the man who was to be the first significant influence on his later career as a racing driver. This was Ian Scott Watson, who remembers meeting Jim for the first time in 1953 at a meeting of the Ednam and District Young Farmers. When asked what first struck him about Jim, Ian recalls being overtaken while driving to the meeting by a Sunbeam Talbot being driven by a 'bloody idiot' who went shooting past him 'like a dose of salts'. According to his memory, he wasn't exactly crawling along, either. When he arrived at the meeting he saw the Sunbeam Talbot in the car park and he asked who the idiot was. It was Jim Clark and the two got talking and before long they had become firm friends. They were both interested in cars and in motor racing and soon Jim was helping Ian at racing events in which Ian was participating.

Ian was farming at Harelaw near Greenlaw at the time but was living on his brother's farm to the south of Kelso at Easter Softlaw. It was the next farm but one from James Clark's at Kerchesters.

Right: Jim with his Border Collie Sweep.

Below: Jim in the ring at the Kelso ram sales in September 1963 just five days after clinching the F1 World Championship.

Jim joined the Berwick and District Motor Club soon after Ian.
At this time, what struck Ian was how quickly Jim took to driving at speed.
Although he was interested in motorsport, Jim probably had no intention
back then of becoming a racing driver. For a young farmer such as him
there were plenty of competitions that he could take part in – such as
rallying, sprints, hill climbing and autocross – but these were essentially
social events. Farmers tend to be mechanically minded and at this time
most of the Berwick and District Motor Club's members were young
farmers. Many of the competitions they entered were fairly rough and
ready and they were completely different from the high-level events in
which Jim was to make his name. One has only to look at the trophies that
Jim won in these early events to see that they were not so different from
many other local sports in which he could have participated. Nevertheless,
races such as these were essential for any aspiring young driver to hone his
skills and race craft if he were to develop into a serious racing driver.

Jim took part in the Border Rally, which – although it was organised
by the club – was a serious event. He quickly demonstrated that he was
equally adept on the off-road sections – which were on farm tracks that
had no speed restrictions – and on the navigation stages on public roads.
Other rallies were like this but Ian reckoned that the Border Rally was
harder-going and a real test of skill and nerve. He proudly recalls that
there was one stage on which he managed to outperform everyone, even
Jim – that's high praise considering Jim was only just starting to race.

There wasn't really any track to follow but Jim had been along the
route beforehand in a Land Rover to recce it and give himself an idea of
what to expect. The drivers were set an average speed of 40M.P.H for this
stage, which Ian initially reckoned was 'unobtainable'. However, he and
his navigator, John Sutherland-Ross, managed it with two seconds to
spare. No one – not even Jimmy – came within ten minutes of this time.

Autocross was just developing as a motorsport activity in the fifties.
It usually just consisted of rough courses marked out on grassy fields and
each race would be run over no more than two or three laps. Ian recalls
one event, in 1954, for which the MG Car Club laid out a figure-of-eight
circuit with a crossing point in the centre. In this event he was driving a
home-made kit car, which was not particularly quick, and Jim was in his
Sunbeam. The drivers were released by the organisers in pairs on two-
or three-lap races. On their race, Jim was so much quicker than Ian that
he ended up half a lap ahead of him and, much to their consternation
at the time – and Ian's amusement now – they met on the intersection.
Fortunately the moment passed without mishap.

Today, hill climbs seem quite a quaint form of competition. Even the
most underpowered of family cars is going to make it up most gradients.
But it was not like that in the fifties. Cars were less powerful back then

and the roads they raced on were less-than-pristine metalled surfaces. Throughout Britain, these events attracted crowds and many of the competitors were up-and-coming racing drivers. Stirling Moss, for instance, was a keen exponent of the form. Indeed the author vaguely remembers that in the sixties some events were so popular that they warranted television coverage, which was still a rare thing for motor racing even at the highest levels.

However, the hill climbs that the Berwick club was organising were, according to Ian, not very 'serious' events. He recalls that the club used to organise one hill climb in the Lammermuirs on public roads, quite illegally without any permission. The drivers were supposed to do their runs at exactly the same time and he and Jim thought that the only way to achieve this was to go flat out from the word 'go'.

The next best things to racing were the sprints at Winfield, a former R.A.F. base about six miles from Jim's home at Edington Mains, or Stobs Camp near Hawick. These were flat-out timed sprints along a straight track marked out by bales of hay. From the beginning, Jim excelled at these events and Ian could see that he was very skilled at driving at speed.

Jim would seem to slow down suddenly, even though the road appeared clear. His eyesight was so acute that he would have spotted a potential hazard, such as a tractor on a side road – possibly even a mile off – and would be taking action to reduce the risk of coming to grief.

Although these sorts of competitions were not, strictly speaking, motor racing, they formed an extremely important apprenticeship for Jim in his development as a racing driver. He had been driving on the farm since he was a child and the operating principles of driving a car were second nature to him before he got his driving licence at seventeen. Competing against his friends taught him how to drive fast and with precision over a variety of surfaces and in different weather conditions.

Ian quickly recognised Jim's skill behind a steering wheel. Although his first experience of Jim's driving on the way to Ednam might have seemed a little reckless, he soon learned that Jim was no harum-scarum type. He describes Jim's road sense as very finely tuned, even in those early days. For instance, he remembers that Jim would seem to slow down

Jim and his mentor and friend Ian Scott Watson with their heads under a car bonnet.

suddenly, even though the road appeared clear: Jim's eyesight was so acute that he would have spotted a potential hazard in the making, such as a tractor on a side road – possibly even as far as a mile off – and he would be taking action to reduce the risk of coming to grief.

In 1955 Jim took part in the International Scottish Rally, held over 1,200 miles of country roads, with Billy Potts, Jim's cousin and another farmer from the Borders. Potts had entered an Austin Healey 100 with Jim as navigator. Jim described this rally as being just as much a social event as it was a sporting competition. After four days of rallying, Jim was given the chance to drive – it was quite normal in those days for the driver and navigator to share the driving. Jim took the opportunity with a vengeance. As they entered Glencoe they were passed by a similar Healey. The racer in Jim came to the fore and he began to push the speed up towards 100M.P.H. and then to about 110M.P.H. at which point Billy Potts' nerve broke. He remembers shouting 'For God's sake . . . Jim, steady'. But he relaxed when he saw 'he was an absolute natural. He had the car completely in his grasp'. Magnanimously he let Jim drive from then on.

Jock McBain, whose Ford dealership was close to Jim's farm, was another strong influence on his early racing career. In this photograph of Border Reivers' silverware he is second from the right with Jim's brother-in-law Alec Calder far right. Ian Scott Watson is to the left, beside Jim.

Chapter 2
A First Taste of Glory

SO FAR AS THE NINETEEN-YEAR-OLD Jim was concerned, he was just having fun racing, nothing more. He'd known since childhood that his role was to run the farm. Messing about in rallies and other local motorsport events was normal for a lad his age but that was that. In fact, after winning his first Formula 1 World Championship, Clark remembered that, 'I entered motor racing as a curiosity. I wanted to see what it was like.'

Ian Scott Watson says he knew even back then that Jim could be world champion but that he thought it was wishful thinking. Jim was quick and very skilful, but rallying is not racing. It is very difficult to excel in rallying but track racing requires a different set of skills and Jim didn't run in a 'proper' race until the summer of 1956.

Jim often tagged along when Ian was racing and, although he was not a mechanic, helped to set up the car. They often talked about the idea that Jim might race but he was reluctant. It wasn't that he was frightened; in fact, he seemed keen. But he knew his parents wouldn't approve and he took his responsibilities towards his family seriously.

Everything changed after he and Ian went up to a race meeting organised by the Aberdeen and District Motor Club at Crimond on 16 June 1956. As usual Jim was along as a mechanic but Ian had quietly entered Jim as a reserve driver with a view to his taking part in the less-important sportscar race. The programme for the meeting, which featured

cars and motorcycles, has the pair entered for two races under the banner of 'Ecurie Agricole'. The drivers are listed as I. Scott Watson and J. Clark Junior. Crimond was in the north-east of Scotland, a good distance from Berwickshire, and there seemed no chance that Jim's parents would find out about it.

One interested spectator that day was a young mechanic and would-be racing driver, George Gordon, who worked for the Ecurie Ecosse driver John Lawrence. He doesn't particularly remember Jim from the race but he does recall two young men from the Borders, dressed in overalls and sporting 'bonnets', every inch the young farmers going motor racing. Jim was officially the mechanic but he and Ian were working together to get the D.K.W. ready to race.

The first three cars home were Lotuses. Colin Chapman's Lotus car company based in north London was already making quite a mark for the serious racer and sportscar aficionado operating on limited financial means but with a penchant for building kit cars. It was to prove crucial to Jim's career, too. The second Lotus to finish was operating under the moniker of the 'Border Reivers', another name that was to become closely linked with Jim's success. Like Ecurie Agricole it was a 'nom de guerre' rather than anything that resembled a professional motor racing team.

It was naive of Jim to think he could keep his racing quiet; word of it reached home long before he did. One of his cousins from Fife, another James Clark, had been at Crimond and had telephoned Kerchesters and told Mr Clark that 'Jim did well today'. James Clark Senior had thought Jim was home at Edington working on the farm and was most displeased to hear of his son's exploits. It wasn't that he was worried by the idea of Jim's racing – after all, it was quite normal for a farmer's son – but it wasn't what Jim was supposed to be spending his time doing.

Although the race at Crimond was Jim's first real test against other racing drivers and undoubtedly wetted his appetite, he saw it as just another day's sport. He still didn't see himself becoming a racing driver.

His next outing, in the same car, was at Beadnell in Northumberland, where a local racing club was carrying out an R.A.C. appraisal of the circuit. R.A.C. observers were present and the event was run much like

Opposite: Jim and Ian at Charterhall in Berwickshire. Ian was clerk of the course which meant he had less time to drive but it gave Jim opportunities to drive Ian's cars.

Above: Jim working on his tractor at home. He was not really mechanically minded but like most farmers he was capable of routine jobs.

a race meeting. Everyone was having a great time until the police turned up to call a halt to proceedings. It transpired that although most of the land belonged to the Duke of Northumberland, one section had been passed over to the R.A.C. on the condition that when it was derequisitioned it should revert to farmland and nothing else. Furthermore, the Duke was chairman of the Lord's Day Observance Society and it was Sunday.

The Scott Watson charm prevailed. He promised that any money raised would be given to charity and the police saw that no one meant any harm. There was only about an hour left to run, so they were allowed to finish.

Jim also had access to more professional racing. The circuit at Charterhall, a converted airfield near Greenlaw not dissimilar to Silverstone, hosted international events. Giuseppe Farina, the first FI World Champion of the modern era, had driven there and Reg Parnell and Stirling Moss were well-known competitors there. But it was very hard to develop the circuit as a serious venue because it was too easy for the public to enter for free and the facilities for cars and spectators were very basic.

The grid markings on the main straight can still be seen on the asphalt now, although the surface is very pot-holed. According to Ian, it wasn't too different back then. The drivers may have been world-class but the venue offered only good-quality club racing.

One of the local luminaries was Jock McBain, the owner of a garage much frequented by the Clarks for their business and motoring needs. He was also a very skilled racing driver and had driven down south on a number of racetracks. He had been the driving force behind the use of Winfield circuit six miles south of Edington Mains and Charterhall and had been able to encourage the top drivers to race in Scotland. However, he had overstretched himself financially and had to relinquish control of Charterhall to the Lothian Car Club.

Jock wanted to form a proper motor racing club with access to Charterhall. The Winfield Joint Committee initially refused but they later relented and allowed the group to organise a club racing event to take place in October 1957. Ian Scott Watson was installed as secretary of the newly formed Border Motor Racing Club (B.M.R.C., which is now the Scottish Motor Racing Club) with Jim as his assistant.

Jim raced in that first meeting at Charterhall. It was his first track race since Crimond sixteen months before so no one could reasonably expect much from him. A week before the race Ian purchased a Porsche 1600, previously owned by the band leader Billy Cotton, which he entered with Jim as the driver because, as the secretary of the meeting, he could not take part himself. Jim ran in three races and finished third and second in the first two, but it was the final race, for the B.M.R.C. Trophy, that really drew attention to his talent. He was up against Jock McBain, an experienced racer in a Raymond May-tuned Ford Zephyr that was much quicker than the Porsche, which was really only a road car. Raymond May was co-founder of the English Racing Automobiles (E.R.A.) racing team – Jock had the better car and the more experienced preparation.

At the off, Jock powered away from the start line. The main straight was just over a mile long and suited his more powerful car which, in theory, should have won every time unless it was hit by unreliability. By the time Jock reached the first corner he was well in the lead and pulling away from Jim. However, around the back of the circuit Jim's now-legendary smooth

Lap after lap the lead changed around the back of the circuit and on the main straight. Each time Jim exited the final bend he was slightly farther ahead until he had enough of a lead to reach the flag ahead.

driving style began to eat into Jock's lead and by the time they came around the final bend Jim was in the lead. Down the main straight Jock put on the power and caught up, getting back into the lead before the first corner. Lap after lap the lead changed around the back of the circuit and again on the main straight. But each time Jim exited the final bend he was slightly farther ahead of Jock until, by the final lap, he had stretched out enough of lead to reach the chequered flag ahead. It was his first win.

It may have been only the first-ever B.M.R.C. meeting at Charterhall but its significance was profound. According to Ian, Jock had tried everything he knew to pull away from Jim but it was all to no avail. Moreover, this was the first time that Jim had ever driven a rear-engined car. Neither he nor Ian had had any experience of driving a car like this one, pushed along by an engine at the rear instead of being pulled by one in the front. The car must have handled very differently and felt unlike anything that Jim was used to, yet he had been able not only to adapt but to outdrive a seasoned racing driver who was in a more powerful car. For someone as inexperienced as Jim was, it requires a lot of luck as well as skill to win, but to beat someone of Jock's calibre was a mighty feat.

Alec Calder, Jim's brother-in-law, was a marshal that day and Ian thinks he later told the family just how good Jim was. What's more, he believes that Jock contacted Jim's father to say that Jim could go far in racing. And according to Jim's sister Betty, Reg Parnell – Aston Martin team manager – told Jim's father that Jim could one day be world champion. Reg was another man who would soon push Jim's motor racing career forward.

Although it was Jim's first win in a competitive race he does not seem to have taken much notice of it. In *Jim Clark at the wheel,* the autobiography he wrote with journalist Graham Gauld in 1964, he commented, 'I remember very little save lapping a farmer friend, Jimmy Somervail, in his Zephyr.' It was typical of Jim not to make much of it or see it as a turning point. During his first two seasons of racing against professional drivers, in 1958 and 1959, he lacked confidence in himself and Ian believes this was the greatest thing holding him back.

The following week Jim and Ian were summoned to Jock's garage in Chirnside, where Jock told them he wanted to reform the Border Reivers racing team with Jim as one of the drivers and Ian as the team manager.

They took the Jaguar off the lorry and Ian led Jim in convoy. It is hard to imagine any driver now who was going to race the next day spending what remained of the night asleep in his manager's car.

Jock had persuaded the fellow directors of his company to purchase a second-hand Jaguar D-type, similar to that used by Ecurie Ecosse.

As far 1957 went, that was about it for Jim Clark as a racing driver, though he ran some sprints at Winfield after the Charterhall meeting. Over the winter Jim was much more concerned with life on the farm than with any daydreams he may have had about being a racing driver.

From 1958, though, Jim was part of a racing team, albeit an amateur one composed mostly of young farmers with a passion for racing. Ian recalls that he was given a free hand to enter the team – and Jim – in whatever races he thought were likely to be productive. He was now in effect Jim's manager and would be until almost the end of 1960.

Jock's influence lay in more than just providing capital and the facilities to set up cars for races. He had been a regular fixture on the British motor racing scene in the south since before the Second World War. Though he had never been a champion in the making he had many influential contacts that were going to serve Jim well as his career developed.

We tend to think of Jim as the team's main driver but that wasn't the intention, although it quickly became the reality because there was only one other person who was keen to drive – Jimmy Somervail – and his farming commitments left more and more of the driving to Jim, who had a more-than-able deputy at Edington in Bill Campbell. Somervail was actually quite an experienced driver and had driven an E.R.A. grand prix car under the Border Reivers banner before the E.R.A. team was closed.

Jim's reputation really began to take off in 1958. Despite increasing opposition from his family he managed to spend less time on the farm and more on racing. He drove in forty-two races at seventeen meetings between April and Boxing Day. As was typical for that period, they were of a great variety of types and standards of competition and all the while Jim was demonstrating his talents to a much wider audience. Even as a novice at the higher levels he was winning almost fifty per cent of his races.

He started the season by racing the Jaguar D-type at Full Sutton, a former American Air Force base in Yorkshire. The meeting fell during a period of cold weather and got off to a shaky start for Jim. The Reivers were using a lorry from his farm to transport the Jaguar and the lorry's radiator had recently been drained because of frost. When Bill refilled it, he turned the taps to close them but, unfortunately, they were already closed and he was actually leaving them open. Jim set off in the lorry behind Ian, in the Porsche. Naturally they did not get beyond Berwick.

Being determined characters, they refused to be deterred by this. They took the Jaguar off the lorry and Ian led Jim most of the way in convoy, Jim driving the Jaguar and leaving the poor lorry abandoned for another day. The lights on the D-type, which was a sportscar designed for racing, were not really up to running on the public road and Ian was performing the role of pathfinder. It is hard to imagine any racing driver today, at anything other than the most basic level of the sport, doing the same thing. Nor would someone who was going to drive in a race the following day spend what remained of the night asleep in his manager's road car.

The following day Jim won his first two races and became the first British driver to average more than 100 M.P.H. in a sportscar race.

After this, Jim drove in two local events – a sprint at Winfield and some more track racing at Charterhall – before the next great career milestone.

For 18 May Ian had entered Jim in two races at Spa in Belgium, the second of which was the 1,000 KM race, one of the more prestigious races on the European calendar. This had come about by chance. Some time during the previous year Ian had had the Porsche serviced in Edinburgh and had met the owner of a Porsche Carrera that was also in the garage. They got talking over coffee and it transpired that Ian's new friend was a keen sportscar driver. He persuaded Ian to consider entering Spa.

David Murray, the owner of Ecurie Ecosse, got wind of this and tried to persuade Jock that Jim was too inexperienced for this type of race. He was undoubtedly right for, although he had the skill, Jim had done very little track racing. So by way of compromise Ian, Jock and Murray agreed that Jim should be shown around the circuit by Jack Fairman, an experienced Ecurie Ecosse driver. They also decided that the two teams would share a garage and help each other during the meeting.

Archie Scott Brown, a legendary Scottish racing driver and one of Jim's heroes.

Ecurie Ecosse were already legends of Scottish motorsport and had employed many renowned drivers, including Masten Gregory and Archie Scott Brown. To Jim, these drivers were heroes, men he hoped to emulate. Scott Brown was a particularly interesting character: despite having a withered arm he was one of the greatest Scottish drivers of the fifties.

Spa-Francorchamps was a long road circuit almost nine miles in length set in the Ardennes, heavily wooded and impossible to marshal properly. There were no escape routes and Jim likened it to racing on a high railway embankment. It was, and still is, is a great test of driver skill and bravery. Jim, although he would be very successful at Spa – winning four consecutive Belgian Grands Prix there – later came to hate this track. If he had known what it was like he might not have agreed to enter.

Fairman took Jim around the track the day before the race, showing him braking points and, in rather macabre fashion, pointing out where fatal accidents had happened. Although it was done with the best intentions this was not really the thing to do to a driver taking his first steps in international competition. Also, as Ian recalls, 'Jimmy was not all that excited by Jack's driving. He kept telling him to go slowly but Jimmy thought he could go quicker.'

Sadly, Ian was unable to stay for the race because he received word that his father was dying and had to fly home. Apart from the personal tragedy, he was left in quandary over how he was to fulfil his obligation to write a race report for *Autosport* magazine. With Jim's help afterwards he was able to piece together the sequence of events and he laughs about it now, saying, 'Nobody twigged'.

For his first international race Jim took a very cautious approach. Modern drivers, some of whom drive in grands prix by this age, have the opportunity to develop their racing skills in karting. Jim had had no such chance because those competitions did not exist in the fifties. Although he was very inexperienced, his innate driving skills meant that he was by no means out of his depth as a driver. Once he had a feel for the track he upped his pace to something approaching 170–180 M.P.H. But he was about to experience tragedy on the racetrack for the first time.

Jim was racing in about eighth place, having just been lapped by Gregory and Scott Brown, who were competing for the lead. They were running just ahead of him on the track when the accident happened. It had started raining on the previous lap and Scott Brown seems to have slid off on a particularly wet corner. As he came around a bend, Jim saw something lying on the track. He didn't know what had happened but he saw a marshal leap out in front of him, waving to slow him down. Another marshal came onto the track and the two of them dragged Scott Brown off to the side of the course.

Understandably, at the end of the race Jim was in a state of shock. It was his first sight of death on the racetrack. He knew that accidents, including fatal ones, were an occupational risk for racing drivers but coming face to face with death, at such close quarters, was a new experience for him. His initial reaction was that motor racing was not for him. He had no desire to be involved in a sport in which people were killed.

As he became more famous Jim was asked to perform more and more in public. Here he is starting and finishing a race (with a Scottish saltire replacing the chequered flag) at Ingliston race track near Kelso in the Scottish Borders.

Jim later recalled in *Jim Clark at the Wheel* that he had only met Scott Brown the day before the race, although he had seen him race the previous year at Charterhall. Ian, however, remembers that Jim and himself had actually met him at his Cambridge garage not long before the race. Like others he was a great admirer of Scott Brown's driving and his ability to control the powerful Lister-Bristol with only one good arm.

After Spa Jim drove in a variety of races over the summer. He raced a number of times in Scotland at his old haunts Stobs Camp, Charterhall and Crimond. He also broadened his profile in England, racing again at Full Sutton on two occasions and Mallory Park and Silverstone in August. At Silverstone he had driven for the Porsche team in the Sixth Hours Handicap Relay Race, finishing twenty-second. He was generally more successful in Scotland, on tracks that he knew, but trying his hand in England was improving his skills and gradually increasing his confidence.

Jock and Ian started turning their thoughts to the following season. Jock was thinking that the Reivers should acquire a single-seater racing car to compete in Formula 2 and they decided to look into buying a Lotus.

Colin Chapman had formed Lotus in the late forties and had been producing innovative designs. As well as being an engineer and racing car designer Colin was a highly skilled racer who had driven the previous year

for Vanwall in Formula 1. His company was run on a shoe-string and his racing ambitions were underwritten by road car sales. He was already an important figure in British racing and was building a grand prix team with a stable of works drivers: Innes Ireland, Cliff Allison and Graham Hill.

As Jim once said, much later, 'Colin is a hard taskmaster . . . Many a time I've seen him talk mechanics into doing what they genuinely think is impossible. But somehow he fires them with his own tremendous enthusiasm . . . If necessary, he'll roll up his sleeves and lend a hand and I think people respect him for that.'

'Many a time I've seen Colin Chapman talk mechanics into doing what they genuinely think is impossible. But somehow he fires them up with his own tremendous enthusiasm.' — Jim Clark

Jock arranged for Jim to try the Lotus 16 at Brands Hatch in October while he was down in the London area to be best man at a friend's wedding. Ian remembers that the whole works team was present, as were Mike Costin, who was developing the Elite car, and five other potential customers. This was not what Ian and Jim had expected – they had assumed that it would just be them and some people from the Lotus team.

It was Jim's first time in a single-seater and he had to orientate himself behind the wheel before driving off. In *Jim Clark at the Wheel* he described almost making a mess of the first corner. Despite the poor start, however, Ian remembers that within five laps Jim was lapping within about two seconds of the works drivers, who knew the Lotus 16 from driving it during its development. Colin began to hop around in agitation, asking, 'Who is this guy? Why have I not seen him before? This is incredible.'

Ian's reply was almost too casual: 'It's all right – he's been driving a Jaguar D-type all season but he's not bad for a wee laddie who's never driven a single-seater before.' Colin Chapman went from one extreme to the other, from being in awe of the way this unknown was swooping around the circuit in his new car to panic. He called Jim in. It turned out to be a blessing in disguise: Hill went out in the car and within two laps the rear suspension collapsed and the wheel and strut flew up into a tree, where they were found the next day. If Jim had been driving he might have been blamed. As a works driver, Graham was very familiar with the car and was able to explain what had actually caused the accident.

Opposite: Jock McBain chatting to Jim in the Lotus 18 Formula Junior car at Charterhall in 1960.

Typically, Ian turned this to their advantage. All the other potential customers had had ten laps in the Lotus 16 whereas Jim had had only five. In compensation, Ian convinced Chapman to give Jim a drive in the Elite.

When he clambered out of the Elite, Jim was grinning from ear to ear. He thought the Elite was far better than the 16. Ian then had, in his own words, a 'mental aberration': if Jim would buy the Porsche from Ian, then Ian would buy an Elite for Jim to race in but also for use as a road car.

Motor racing was such a very small world that Colin remembered Ian as the Scot who had backed out of buying a Lotus VI because it meant paying up front and then waiting three or four months for the car. He knew of Ian but had never heard of Jim, even though Jim had been driving the D-type all year. The Jaguar was a faster car than the Lotus 16 but at this stage Colin was unwilling to take a risk on this young unknown driver.

The aim of visiting the testing session had been to obtain a vehicle that would take Jim and the Reivers to a higher level of competition. Jim hadn't been that impressed with the Lotus 16's handling and the mechanical failure had convinced him and Ian that it was not worth driving. Ian had bought the Elite, but that was not the car that the Reivers were looking for. Jock then decided that they needed to purchase a Lister Jaguar, a car that had been outperforming the D-type all season.

The visit also gave Jim his first chance to speak with Colin. Afterwards, Jim described him as an easy man to talk to, someone who was eager to discuss ideas for racing cars. It would be too far-fetched to state that their friendship began at this meeting but obviously Colin had made a big impression on Jim while he stood watching other drivers test the car.

Colin was to get a closer view of Jim's racing skills before the year was out. Ian remembers that Colin was very supportive and encouraging: he may not have been willing to take a risk with his precious Formula 2 car but he was willing to put opportunities in Jim's path and see how the young man from the Borders handled them. Colin told Ian that the Elite would be ready in time for him to enter Jim in the Boxing Day meeting at Brands Hatch. Ian agreed and on Christmas Day he and Jim travelled down to London overnight by train, picking up the Elite in the morning and driving out to the circuit to practise for the race.

For much of the race, Jim and Colin were closely matched, but then Jim began to pull away. Just before the end, however, Jim was delayed by a backmarker, allowing Colin to pass him and win. According to Ian it was this great duel that led Colin to decide that he wanted Jim in his cars.

George Campbell remembers that Jim was still quite content with being a farmer. He was still driving a combine harvester full-time during the harvest season. Gradually, however, Jim asked George increasingly often if he would take over and let Jim get away early to go racing.

In 1959 Jim drove the Lister in sportscar races and the Lotus Elite in the *Autosport* GT Championship. He also had the odd outing in what was now his own Porsche 1600. Jim described the Lister as 'fun' and 'a beast' that taught him a lot about racing. He also had the car modified to suit his style: part of the bulkhead behind the seats was removed to allow him to have the driver's seat pushed back. It had more responsive acceleration than the D-type and the brakes required capable handling if they were not to overheat. He soon became skilled at setting it up for corners and using the acceleration to bring around the car's tail.

The year's racing featured a number of familiar circuits, particularly in Scotland, where he sprinted at Stobs Camp and Winfield and raced at

Jim after winning the *Autosport* 3-hour race at Snetterton in 1959. Ian Scott Watson, who owned the Lotus Elite which Jim drove, is on his right shoulder.

Previous pages:
Three Lotus Elites at
scrutineering for the 1959
Le Mans 24-hour Race.
Jim Clark's and John
Whitmore's Elite is in the
foreground. Jim was
placed 3rd overall in the
1960 race.

Charterhall. And a greater number of his races were against higher quality fields in more prestigious events.

His season started on 30 March at Mallory Park, where he raced four times and won all four races. He then had three races in three weeks at Oulton Park and Aintree without success, but then it was back to Charterhall on 25 April, where he had two more successes from three races as he began to get the hang of the Lister.

The highlight of this first part of the season was undoubtedly his first attempt at the Le Mans 24 Hours. This race has a cachet all of its own, perhaps rivalled only by America's Indianapolis 500. It is in a sense not so much a race as a test of reliability and endurance. To perform well, you need a strong car with a driver who can drive smoothly and quickly without overtaxing his vehicle with unnecessary high revving.

Ian had bought the Elite with intention that he would drive it over the winter and Jim would drive it during the season. At Oulton Park one of the rear suspension struts had been pushed through the mounting point and Ian was unwilling to let it race at Le Mans without a proper repair.

Instead, he did a deal with Colin, who would provide another Elite for them to use at Le Mans. The original car was actually a pre-production model and the one to be supplied for the race would have a strengthened rear suspension. Colin and Ian agreed that Ian could have first refusal on the car if it survived the race intact and that Colin could pick Jim's co-driver. He chose John Whitmore, a talented sportscar driver until the mid-sixties, when he became completely disenchanted with the sport.

Whitmore also had a pre-production Elite and had impressed Colin when racing against him at the *Daily Express* meeting at Silverstone in May. Just like Jim had done at Brands Hatch, Whitmore had raced against Colin in an Elite and put up a good race before losing out in the end.

Before they set off for France, the Reivers contacted Lotus and were told that the car was ready to be collected. Jock and Colin Clark (who was unrelated to Jim) went down with the Bedford transporter, only to find that the Lotus mechanics were still busy putting the engine in the car.

The Reivers had already been given the chassis details for the permit that they needed to export the car but the Elite that Jock eventually turned up with had the wrong chassis number. Ian was, he says, 'nonplussed'. He believes Colin must have taken the car out for a test drive over the weekend and written it off but been unwilling to admit it. Apparently the list kept by Warren King, chief clerk of Lotus, shows that chassis 1036 – the one that Jock was supposed to collect – was never sold. The actual car collected was chassis number 1035.

Whatever the truth of the matter, the Reivers had to complete the car's assembly at Le Mans. To do this they had to take thirty-two boxes and crates with them. It was an incredible feat given that Jock was their only mechanic and he was the garage owner so had little time to get his hands dirty. The rest of the guys were farmers, although some of them, such as Jim's brother-in-law Alec, were very capable mechanics.

They got the Elite into race order and into the capable hands of Jim and Whitmore, who had it running at twenty seconds a lap quicker than the other Elites. The drivers of the other 1,220cc Elites thought the Reivers must be running a 1,500cc engine and wanted the scrutineers to strip down the car. The Reivers avoided this by comparing their car to the 1,500 being driven by Innes Ireland.

Ian reckons this Elite was the most reliable car the Reivers ever raced, despite its having a faulty rev counter. The optimum for economical and fast racing was 7,000R.P.M. but the mechanical rev counter was reading about 500R.P.M. too low so for most of the twenty-four hours the engine was actually operating at 7,500R.P.M. on the straights – the absolute maximum the Coventry Climax engine could cope with.

Jim with Jabby Crombac, the French motoring journalist in the pit lane. Jim lived with Jabby in a flat in Paris whilst a temporary tax exile.

Back then, the Le Mans started with the drivers sprinting across the track and leaping into their cars. Moss was regarded as the past master at this type of race start but all he had to do was run and then leap into his car. Jim was also very athletic but he had to get into the Elite and then shut the door before he could pull out, potentially losing valuable seconds. Even so, their cars started moving at the same time.

There wasn't really any race strategy as such. The Reivers' aim was to keep the car running as long as possible, with both men getting an equal share of the driving. The starter motor shaft broke twice during the race, probably because of a vibration caused by running at 7,500R.P.M. Pitstops became problematic because the team was never quite sure whether the car would start easily afterwards. This provided a bit of a dilemma for the Reivers because under the Le Mans rules any replacement parts had to be carried on the car and they had not brought a spare starter motor. They started stretching the spells between stops to minimise the number of times they'd have to restart the car.

Luckily for them Jabby Crombac, the French motoring journalist, Lotus enthusiast and friend of Colin, had entered his Elite. His car's timing slipped and the exhaust overheated, setting fire to the upholstery. The driver immediately pulled over in front of the pits at Mulsanne corner and leapt out. Before the race, he had been very concerned about the fibreglass bodywork catching fire but Chapman had convinced him that the Elite had a self-extinguishing material to counter this danger. So the driver simply took off his helmet and gloves, laid them on the driver's seat and waited for the fire to go out. Ian recalls that by the time the flames were extinguished parts of the engine had begun to melt and the rest of the car had to be shovelled up into dustbins.

The silver lining of all this for the Reivers was that Jabby's mechanic was Lotus's chief mechanic. He had a socket set with seven joints that enabled him to get into the starter motor without having to remove the manifold. Luckily it was dark when his assistance was needed so he told the Reivers mechanics to line up with a gap in the middle. He removed the starter motor, juggled it around as if it were hot and then seemed to drop it over the back of the car. He then produced the new starter motor and opened it. Ian fiddled with some brushes and announced that they were the problem and appeared to carry out repairs. They attached the motor and off the car went, the Le Mans officials hopefully tricked by the ruse.

Unfortunately they had the same problem again later, when it was light. This time Jabby's mechanic asked the Reivers to get a pail of soapy water with the new starter motor hidden in it. The old part really was hot when it came off because they wasted no time in removing it. The guys proceeded to 'clean' the starter motor, removing the replacement part from its hiding place. This all went on in front of the French official responsible for ensuring that they kept to the rules. He slapped Ian on the back exclaiming, 'Very good acteeng', and Ian reckons they got away with it only because they were a Scottish team and not the official Lotus entrant.

Despite spending more than two hours in the pits Jim and Whitmore finished strongly. They competed in the 1,500cc category but their lap times averaged less than five minutes and they came tenth overall and second in their class – a very good performance for a first drive at Le Mans. It hadn't been Jim's usual sort of racing and was somewhat out of character because getting the pace right is paramount in endurance racing. Jim's preferred style of starting fast and pulling away fast was more likely cause problems in such a race by putting too much strain on the car.

Whitmore certainly enjoyed himself at Le Mans. He found the Reivers to be a keen bunch. What they lacked in professionalism they more than made up for in commitment: Ian was responsible for the Porsche and Lotus Elite expenses while Jock took care of the D-type, Lister and Aston Martin costs. McBain's garage was responsible for setting up the cars for racing. Jock put up most of the money for their race entry and the others put in a lot of hard work. Similarly, the Reivers were obviously appreciative of John's efforts because, later in the season, he drove for them again, in the Lister Jaguar at Charterhall.

In August Jim had his one and only race for Ecurie Ecosse, the premier Scottish motor racing team of the fifties. It was the Tourist Trophy at Goodwood, which Jim drove with Masten Gregory, who was his number-one hero at the time. They were driving the Ecurie Ecosse's Tojeiro Jaguar. Ian reckons this was a turning point in Jim's career because it enabled him to compare his own performance against that of one of his heroes in the same car. Jim drove the first stint, then handed the Tojeiro over to Masten with the car running in fourth place. What he saw next completely changed his mind about his abilities.

Standing with Ian in the pits, Jim watched Masten dropping back down the field. 'I can't understand it,' he said. 'Everyone's going so slowly.' Ian's reply was, 'Don't be an idiot – it's you who's been going so fast.'

Up until this point, Jim had just considered himself a good driver with good equipment. At Spa the previous year, for instance, he had been driving very quickly – up to 170R.P.M. on the straights – but Gregory had just blown past him as if he were crawling along and because of this Jim had developed a lot of respect for him. So when he outperformed Gregory at Goodwood the scales finally dropped from Jim's eyes.

This new-found belief couldn't help the team in the Tourist Trophy, though, because Masten lost the car at Woodcote, burying it deep in the bank. Happily for Masten, he leaped out of the car before the impact and escaped with only a broken shoulder. The other incident of note was that Moss's Aston caught fire in the pits while being refuelled. The fuel line was switched on before the cap was taken off and some fuel sprayed onto the hot exhaust pipe, torching the car and part of the pits. Stirling leapt into the other Aston and went on to win the race.

Chapter 3
Grand Prix Apprentice

AT THE END OF 1959 JIM WAS still very much a young farmer with an interest in racing, rather than a full-time racing driver. Unlike most of his fellow farmers, however, he was developing a reputation for winning. He was now twenty-three years old and very keen to try his hand at higher levels of the sport, but his family was still strongly against the idea. As with most young people, especially those with a great talent, it was always going to be difficult to hold him in.

Towards the end of the year Jim was approached by Reg Parnell, the Aston Martin team manager, and asked if he wished to drive in Formula 1. Still uncertain about his ability, Jim agreed to test an FI car at Goodwood in January 1960. It would be only the third time that he sat in a single-seater car – and the second was on Boxing Day 1959 at Brands Hatch, where he struggled with an unfamiliar car.

He obviously impressed the Aston Martin team, however, because they soon offered him a second trial. Lotus was also keen to get Jim's signature on a contract and, on the day of the second test, turned up at Goodwood with a Lotus

Below: Competing in a milk float race at Ingliston outside Edinburgh. Jim came 2nd...

Jim in the Lotus 18 (N° 6) alongside Graham Hill's B.R.M. at the 1960 Dutch GP at Zandvoort.

Junior for Jim to drive. He was very impressed by Lotus and the opportunity the team offered but he had already agreed to drive for Parnell and Aston.

So the plan developed for 1960 was for Jim to split his driving between the Reivers, Aston Martin and Lotus. Parnell had him under contract to drive FI for Aston and Colin had Jim for Formula Junior. But things worked out quite differently.

Parnell and Aston soon realised that their car was never going to be competitive. It was essentially a front-engined Maserati clone, a throwback to an era that Colin and others had consigned to the history books with their rear-engined revolution.

Parnell had signed Jim because he recognised in him a driver with huge potential, but he was not the type of man to stand in a driver's way. He had already agreed with Colin that Jim could help Lotus until the Aston was

ready to race, but by the time of the British Grand Prix in July Aston
Martin had withdrawn from FI and released Jim from his contract.

Jim was not immediately catapulted into the Lotus grand prix team,
however. Colin had plenty of drivers for his cars, one of whom was John
Surtees, the motorcycle world champion. Surtees had successfully made
the jump from motorcycles to single-seater car racing at the highest level
but he was also continuing to compete on bikes and in 1960 this took
precedence over FI. Inevitably the two racing calendars sometimes
clashed, which gave Colin the opportunity to let Jim show what he was
capable of in an FI car.

Jim still had time to drive for the Border Reivers in the Aston Martin
DBRI, twice as co-driver to Roy Salvadori. One of these races was the
1,000KM sportscar race at Germany's Nürburgring in May. He again
beat Stirling Moss in a Le Mans-style start but it was to no avail; he had
to retire before the end of his stint.

Jim is led by his team
mate Innes Ireland at the
1960 Belgian GP.

Previous pages: Jim in his first British GP follows behind Jack Fairman in the Cooper.

Above: The Portuguese GP of 1960, was held on the streets of Oporto. Jim came a cropper in practice when he got his Lotus 18 stuck in the tramlines.

Jim drove in his first F1 grand prix at Zandvoort in the Netherlands on 6 June and was running up in fourth place when the gearbox gave up. Two weeks later he continued this promising start to his F1 career by finishing fifth at Spa in one of the most horrific race weekends of his career: two drivers were killed and one seriously injured. Moss broke both his legs in practice while driving the Rob Walker-owned Lotus. Then during the race Chris Bristow, driving a Cooper, while battling for position with Willy Mairesse in a Ferrari, lost control of his car on the same spot as Moss had and was killed. Soon afterwards, Jim came around the bend and saw two marshals rushing onto the track and waving frantically at him. One of the marshals grabbed Bristow's body and dragged it out of Jim's path.

Jim later said, 'I was almost put off racing completely. I remember at the end of the race finding that my car was spattered with blood.'

Then Jim's team-mate Alan Stacey was hit in the face by a bird, lost control of the car and went off the circuit. His car went up in flames. Motor racing in the fifties and sixties was very dangerous at the best of times but on a high-speed circuit such as Spa there was little margin for error. Jim still remembered seeing Archie Scott Brown's death on his first visit to Spa and it is a testimony to his courage that he did not give up the sport.

The week after Spa, Jim ran his second race with Roy Salvadori in the Border Reivers Aston: the Le Mans 24 Hours. The race was dominated by Ferraris, which took six of the first seven places; the Reivers spoiled their party by coming in third. Jim knew that his usual racing strategy of leading from the start was not a viable tactic at Le Mans but his natural driving technique was a great asset: he was easy on the engine and very assured with all his braking points and turn-in.

After Le Mans, Jim had two grands prix in July: the French at Reims, where he came fifth, and the British at Silverstone, where he suffered suspension trouble that dropped him to sixteenth from third.

Jim's best grand prix drive of the season came at the Portuguese Grand Prix on 14 August. This was held on a street circuit in Oporto. As with many of the circuits on which they raced back then, the F.I.A., motorsport's governing body, would not allow a circuit like this to be used for F1 today. The surface was cobbled and broken up by tramlines, causing a lot of wear and tear on the cars. In practice, Jim got caught out by the tram-

lines, getting his wheels jammed in them. Unable to get free or – therefore
– steer, he crashed through the bales of straw that acted as 'crash barriers'
and hit a lamp post, overturning his car.

It was virtually a write-off, which was a crisis for Colin and the team.
At this point Lotus's cash flow was such that the team was unable to get
its transporter back to Britain unless all three cars received the starting
money, which was paid on all cars that completed three laps of the race.
The Lotus mechanics therefore worked through the night to get Jim's car
ready for the race. Ian recalls that they virtually had to rebuild the car,
straightening out the damaged chassis and gearbox casing. Parts of the
bodywork were held together with masking tape and the car was no longer
racing green but a dirty buff colour.

Jim's instructions from Colin were simply to complete the necessary
laps to receive the starting money. After that it was up to him, but in the
event the car felt so good that Jim stayed out there and managed to finish
third. It was his best finish of the season and a sign of things to come.

In August Bob Dance, a mechanic, joined Lotus. His memories throw
an interesting light on the world that Jim was entering. For instance, Rob
Walker, who ran a private motor team, was a
great friend of Colin's and Bob recalls that it
was not unusual to see him at Lotus team
meetings, which would be unthinkable in
today's world of commercial secrecy and
heightened team rivalries. There was also a
greater bond between drivers: they shared
an almost constant danger of dying on the
circuit and were less in the public limelight,
so the tensions between them seemed less
than those among modern drivers.

Bob's impression of Jim was that he was a
quiet, unassuming person who got on with
the job at hand and that he got fast and
consistent results. He took time to get to
know people and often asked the mechanics
what they knew of new people when they
joined the team.

In fact, Bob summarises those days thus:
'We had the feeling that Jimmy – of course –
was the man capable of winning the races.
Chapman was capable of operating the cars,
Len Terry was very capable of designing the
cars and the lads were very good. Everything
just seemed to click together.'

A good view of Jim's
Lotus 18 at Oporto.
Although a rear-engined
car it looks more like the
earlier front-engined cars
which it superseded.

The Formula Junior
Lotus 18 in which Jim
drove to a share of the
championship in 1960
with his team-mate
Trevor Taylor.

However, FI wasn't Jim's main focus in 1960. His main competitions
were the Formula 2 races, among which he won the Kentish 100 at Brands
Hatch in August, and the Formula Junior championship in which he drove
the Lotus 18 junior version with Trevor Taylor as his team-mate. The
Formula Junior competition can be loosely described as a forerunner of
modern Formula 3 and was a class of competition designed to bring
on younger drivers towards FI. Lotus was very successful in this category
in 1960, with Clark and Taylor dominating the European races, often
finishing first and second.

Racing for the Gold Cup in September at Oulton Park, Jim had his
first big accident when he collided with Brian Naylor, a backmarker, in
a JBW-Maserati. Jim was chasing Innes Ireland and Naylor let Ireland
through but didn't realise Jim was also there and pulled back onto the

racing line, giving Jim no time to avoid him. Jim was very upset and had to be restrained by a marshal to prevent him from hitting Naylor. Even once he got back to his hotel room he couldn't calm down and, despite Ian's best efforts to dissuade him, Jim decided to return to Edington Mains that evening. He set off to drive back alone.

Ian's sleep was disturbed that night when the hotel put a call through to his room. It was from the Lancashire Police, who had a Mr Clark with them who wanted to go home. Jim had come up to a junction and was still so upset by the accident that he couldn't decide which of two forks to take so he went straight on, crashing his car. As a loyal friend and manager, Ian got up and started the trek home to Scotland.

Once he became a full-time driver Jim lacked time to help around the farm. Edington Mains was his home base but really he was living out of a suitcase. He was away virtually all the time and had to leave the farm's management in the hands of Bill Campbell. His visits home were generally for only a few days and George Campbell recalls that Jim would arrange to meet Bill in the farm office to catch up on things and pay bills.

Jim's father was still managing Kerchesters and Over Roxburgh so Jim was completely reliant on Bill to keep Edington Mains on track. He later acknowledged, in *Jim Clark at the Wheel,* just how important this was. If he hadn't had someone so capable and trustworthy at home he might not have taken up full-time racing. It says much about Jim's professional attitude to life that everything was done thoroughly. For instance, he would pay the bills only once he had been through them himself.

Life as a racing driver, even in the early sixties when things were a lot more relaxed and easy-going, involved compromises on normal life. One Christmas Eve, Jim asked George to give him a lift to the station at Berwick. When asked if he was going anywhere special, all Jim would say was that he was testing cars. George puts some of this reticence down to Jim's shyness, but perhaps there was also embarrassment that racing had taken over so much of his life that he was giving up a family Christmas.

Asked now if he could see Jim's potential back then, George says, 'I could never understand how Jim took to it. He never showed it. He liked to go right enough [go fast]. I'd seen him in the sprints. He was really quick but I never thought he could go so far.'

Life would get easier once Jim got a plane, a bit later in life. He could fly up from London in maybe an hour and a half rather than spending hours in a car. For another thing that inevitably had to change over the coming years was that Jim would eventually spend more time in London (staying, from 1962 to 1964, in John Whitmore's flat). Once he had that plane, Jim said there was nothing better than flying over the Cheviot Hills and looking into Scotland. Often the first sign of his arrival was the sight of his aircraft making a few passes over the farm before landing at Winfield,

where he had taken part in some of his early sprints. If he was at home, George Campbell's brother would drive over to Winfield and pick Jim up. Later, Jim put a door on one of the old R.A.F. buildings on the airfield and used it as a garage for a Lotus Cortina so that he could drive himself back to the farm rather than relying on Campbell.

Towards the end of 1960, Jim persuaded Colin to let him drive the Formula Junior Lotus 18 at Charterhall. He was at Oulton Park the day before, where he raced twice with the same car, but it was particularly important to him to race in Berwickshire because this would be his last chance that season. One of his competitors that day was a George Gordon from Aberdeenshire, who had been at Crimond when Jim first raced in 1956. He remembers that Jim was behind him on the grid because of not having participated in practice. He saw Jim only twice during the race, once just after the start when Jim's Lotus 18 powered past his Lotus 7 and then a few laps later when he waved Jim through to lap him. It was only after the race that he learned that Jim had been forced to retire with transmission problems.

Jim began 1961 by competing in the Tasman Series, which was held in Australia and New Zealand during January and February and provided an opportunity for Antipodean fans to see FI cars in action. According to Dance, it also offered a chance for Australian and New Zealander mechanics to be at home for Christmas and the first few weeks of the year. The cars were shipped out via the Cape and the drivers flew out just before the end of the year. Jim took part in three races but didn't particularly distinguish himself, although he did mange to finish second in the Intercontinental race at Levin.

He was now a fully fledged Lotus FI driver and not just a substitute for whenever Surtees was unavailable. There were new regulations for FI in 1961: the cars were not to exceed 1,500cc, the size of F2 in 1960. Furthermore, alcohol and nitro-methane fuel and superchargers were banned. Colin and his fellow British team managers had been unhappy at having these changes sprung on them towards the end of the previous year, having planned to run larger-engined cars. Suddenly they had to start again. There was an undercurrent of suspicion that somehow Ferrari had had some prior warning of what was going on and its car, the 156, was far ahead of the other teams'. For Lotus, it meant starting the year with the successful 1960 F2 car.

It also meant that Lotus would be up against the odds when trying to compete with Ferrari. Driver skill obviously counted for a lot but without a competitive car the odds were greatly lengthened. Jim was determined that, now he was an established Lotus driver, he was going to demonstrate his worth to the team. Whenever he could he was going to hang onto the coat-tails of the Ferraris and take advantage of any slips or retirements that came along. It would be a hard season for him but he was young and eager to succeed and he had the brain to identify his strengths and find ways to make the most of them.

The first European grand prix was a non-championship event at Pau in the Pyrenees. Being a non-championship event, the field was not too great. Jim qualified second, which was particularly good because it was a street circuit with which he was unfamiliar. Jack Brabham was ahead of him on pole and Jim felt it was important to get ahead of Brabham at the start.

Jim holds up fellow Lotus driver Innes Ireland in the hospitality tent after the 1960 *Autosport* 3-hour race. A beaming Ian Scott Watson stands alongside him.

As it turned out, the start of the race was almost comical, being slightly delayed because one of the drivers was missing. Jim's car was there but there was no sign of either him or his mechanics. Raymond Roche, the starter, was shouting and screaming and most of the engines were running while Jim was looking for his gloves. As Jim clambered into his car, Roche signalled with his fingers: five seconds to go. Showing more aplomb and calmness than might have been expected under the circumstances, Jim smoothly out-accelerated Brabham into the first corner.

At the end of the first lap Jim was leading Brabham, who was followed by Jo Bonnier. For the others, the race was already virtually over. Brabham dropped out soon after the start and by lap fifty (out of one hundred) Jim had a lead of fifty-one seconds over Bonnier, who was the only other driver on the same lap. By the end of the race Jim was more than ninety seconds ahead. His only problem came when he switched over to the reserve fuel tank and the engine began to run rough because the fuel was running the wrong way down the line. It soon sorted itself out, however, and Jim took his first grand prix victory. Its brilliance was only slightly marred by the absence of Dan Gurney and the Ferraris against which to gauge the victory.

On 9 April the Brussels Grand Prix was held on the streets to the north of the city around Heysel. Jim qualified on the third row. The race was to run over three heats of twenty-two laps but unfortunately he did not make it beyond the second lap of the first heat because his gearbox broke.

Jim's first full championship season started at Monaco in mid-May. This has always been the most prestigious and glamorous race in F1, the ultimate in street races with a backdrop of celebrities in a tax haven beside the Mediterranean. It held – and still holds – a certain cachet for drivers and teams and is the race to win. It is very demanding of cars and drivers, needing a combination of endurance, skill and mechanical reliability.

Yet Jim was never to win there, no matter how hard he tried and how well-prepared his car. It was not so surprising when he had new cars with teething problems, but in other years it was a puzzle. Other drivers, including Moss, won in Lotus cars. Jim's best opportunity was probably in 1965, when he swept all before him in the early part of the season but the race was the day before the Indy 500, which he and Colin had set their hearts on winning, so Jim didn't compete. Even in 1960, he was leading the Formula Junior race when an ignition lead broke and he came in seventh.

In 1961, Jim crashed at St Devote in practice and badly damaged his Lotus 21. He qualified third but finished last in the race, having spent time in the pits with ignition problems. Speed is not the most important quality at Monaco. Points can be scored by an accurate driver with a good technique that keeps the car running, so being there at the end was a real achievement, especially at his first attempt. The race was won by Moss in a slightly outdated Lotus, which demonstrates the importance of the driver.

A week later, Jim moved onto the Dutch Grand Prix at Zandvoort.
Monaco may have been an unlucky circuit for Jim but Zandvoort was
one of his lucky ones. The competitors for some races were selected by
invitation, with some places reserved for quick qualifiers, and this was how
the Zandvoort field was chosen. It resembled a modern grand prix in that
each team had only two entries – except for Ferrari, which had three, perhaps down to its prestige. The second driver for Lotus was Taylor because
Ireland had crashed at Monaco and fractured his knee.

Jim's car was there but there was no sign of either him or his mechanics. The starter was shouting and screaming and most of the engines were running while Jim was looking for his gloves.

Practice was dominated by the powerful Ferrari drivers Richie Ginther,
Phil Hill and Wolfgang Von Trips. Jim managed the fourth row on the grid,
just a second slower than the leading Ferrari of Phil Hill. He started well,
passing several cars, and ran in fourth and even third place during the
opening laps, able to keep in touch with the leaders. By about one-third
distance he was running third, less than five seconds behind Von Trips.
He held third place to the end and it seemed a very promising omen.

At the end of May Jim took part in the Nürburgring 1,000KM, in which
he drove an Aston-Martin DBR1 with Bruce McLaren as his co-driver under
the banner of Essex Racing, a team with close links to Lotus. Jim had the
first drive and athleticism enabled him to get away first in the Le Mans-style
start but Moss quickly caught and passed him in a Porsche, which was only
to be expected because the DBR1 was a 1959 car that was a little past its
prime. They were running high in the order with McLaren at the wheel
when on the twenty-fourth lap they had to retire with mechanical problems.

Jim also drove the DBR1 at Le Mans for the Border Reivers with Ron
Flockhart as co-driver and Ian running the show. Flockhart had won at
Le Mans twice, in 1956 and 1957, with Ecurie Ecosse, but the DBR1 had
little chance of winning. However, with Jim as first driver, it was no surprise
for them to lead at the start. In his autobiography he described himself as
first into the long Mulsanne straight but seventh out of it. During the night
the team had to abandon the race because the car developed clutch trouble,
which caused a spectacular fire that was – luckily – put out by the wind.

The Belgian Grand Prix was held in mid-June with a field of twenty-five
entrants. Ireland was back in the other Lotus, having recovered from his

The 1961 Dutch GP. Jim is just a dot in the field lying in fourth behind Von Trips who is leading the field round in his Ferrari Dino.

Monaco injuries. The team missed the first day of practice because its cars had not arrived – and when they did turn up things still did not go well because Lotus was experimenting with its car set-ups. Despite the good showing at Zandvoort, Chapman probably felt that their chances were limited so decided to use the time to find a better set-up. As a result, both Lotuses were near the back of the grid, on the seventh row. Jim was over two seconds faster than his team-mate but a massive eighteen seconds behind Phil Hill's Ferrari on pole.

It didn't get any better in the race. Innes retired after nine laps and Jim finished twelfth, six laps behind Hill's Ferrari. His Lotus, which was new, had spent time in the pits when his gear assembly failed on the first lap. Lotus clearly had a lot of work to do to be competitive.

The French Grand Prix at Reims in early July was another tough race, though more profitable than Spa. This was another fast circuit that favoured the Ferraris but Lotus was in the hunt right from the start.

Jim and Innes were well up with the chase but Innes had trouble with his throttle getting jammed open by some gravel that was spraying about at the end of the main straight. He still managed to finish fourth, however. Jim also suffered from this, damaging his teeth and having his goggles disintegrate thanks to the battering they received. The important thing was that he kept going to the end, coming in third. Ferrari, which had an extra car driven by Giancarlo Baghetti, came out on top.

At the British Grand Prix at Aintree Jim qualified eighth but an oil line problem put him out. The top three finishers were Ferraris.

Next up, in August, was the European Grand Prix in Germany. It was won by Moss in Rob Walker's privately owned Lotus 18, which should have been no match for its newer rivals, but Moss was so good that they couldn't keep up. Jim came in fourth, just over a minute behind Moss.

Although Jim had the newer Lotus, this was a fantastic achievement for an inexperienced driver first time out in a grand prix car at the formidable Nürburgring, an incredibly challenging fourteen-mile circuit. The mountainous terrain meant not only that the cars would be climbing and descending throughout the race, but also sometimes having to cope with different weather conditions on each lap.

Jim had seen Archie Scott Brown die in a sportscar race at Spa in 1958 and on the same circuit in 1960 had been present when two others died during the grand prix meeting. But so far he had not been personally involved in a fatal accident. That changed at Monza.

It was possibly an accident in the making all season. The Lotuses had less power than the Ferraris and the team's tactic on the faster circuits was to sit in the Ferraris' slipstreams to keep up with them and then look for opportunities to overtake. This had worked well for Lotus so far, but they had still not won a championship race and it seemed very unlikely that they would do so at Monza.

By this time it looked as though Von Trips would be champion. Jim got ahead of Von Trips in the race but was unable to stay in front. He tucked himself into the Ferrari's slipstream and managed to keep up with the faster car. At the breaking point for the northern of the Lesmo Curves, Von Trips pulled out to overtake someone, which he would surely not have done had he realised that Jim was so close. It left the Lotus nowhere to go and all Jim could do was brake and pray for deliverance.

Unfortunately there was no hope. The cars' wheels touched and they spun off the circuit. Von Trips was thrown out of his car and died instantly on the roadside while his Ferrari was launched into the crowd, killing fourteen spectators. F1 may have been only for the brave, and fatalities in the crowd were not unknown, either, but this was a tragedy of horrific proportions with terrible implications for all concerned.

An unplanned meeting of the Grand Prix Drivers Association at the Belgian GP in Spa 1961 listens to Stirling Moss. The previous year had seen two fatalities on what was a high speed, high risk circuit. Jim is standing with his hands in his pockets. Others present include Jack Brabham, Innes Ireland, Masten Gregory, Phil Hill and Dan Gurney.

The start of the French GP at Reims. Jim is running in 8th place. Richie Ginther leads Phil Hill and Wolfgang Von Trips.

Jim in the Lotus 21 at Aintree during the British GP of 1961.

The law in Italy demands that someone take responsibility for a fatality. Jim's Lotus was impounded. It was not actually all that badly damaged and the team was allowed to remove the engine and gearbox, presumably because they could give no information on the cause of the accident.

Jim was not a man who liked to vocalise his feelings but there was no hiding the fact that the crash had shaken him badly. Colin whisked him away from the circuit – and the Italian police who were keen to interview him – to his private plane. Even back in Berwickshire among familiar faces Jim said very little. Ian remembers that Jim volunteered nothing about his feelings so he didn't ask although he knew that Jim was a friend of Von

Trips'. This how Jim described the accident: '*Von Trips and I were racing along the straightaway and were nearing one of the banked curves . . . We were about 100 metres from the beginning of the curve. Von Trips was running close to the inside of the track. I was closely following him, keeping near the outside. At one point Von Trips shifted sideways so that my front wheels collided with his back wheels. It was the fatal moment. Von Trips' car spun twice and went into the guardrail along the inside of the track. Then it bounced back, struck my own car and bounced down into the crowd*'. Jim would have understood how lucky he was not have gone off the circuit with Von Trips, especially because survival often makes a man much more aware of his mortality than he had been before.

George Campbell recalls Jim's first visit to the farm after the accident. George was working on the combine when Jim drove up, ran the twenty yards to the combine and clambered up the steps. It was obvious to George that he was very cut up and even by Jim's standards he was quiet. He said only that there were problems with the police and he wasn't keen to race at Monza again.

One of his sisters also remembers that Jim was very upset about 'Taffy' Von Trips' death. He did not like to speak about it – he preferred to keep these kinds of issues to himself, but it was a forlorn hope. The press were very keen for a story and photographers kept pestering him on the farm. About a month afterwards, a German couple turned up at Edington and gave Jim a film that demonstrated that the accident was not his fault: he had kept going straight but Von Trips had been unaware of his presence and moved into him.

But life went on and soon it was time to race again. Jim came seventh in the US Grand Prix at Watkins Glen and Ireland steered the Lotus 21 to victory. This was Lotus's first F1 World Championship win and Innes thought that his prospects within the team were very good, yet in only a few weeks he was sacked and Jim was the number-one driver. It is well-known that Innes blamed Jim for conspiring against him; he felt that whenever he entered a room in which Jim was talking with Colin, they stopped and looked at him – a natural reaction when someone enters a room.

Innes was an excellent driver but was, in modern parlance, a party animal. He liked to

The Lotus 21 in much drier conditions at Stuttgart for the Solitude Grand Prix.

Tragedy at Monza, 1961. Following closely behind Von Trips' car, the front wheel of Jim's Lotus touched the Ferrari causing them both to spin off. Von Trips' body can be seen to the left of his car, whilst Jim's comparatively undamaged car lies nearby.

drink and smoke, the antithesis of Jim. Although Innes and Jim were not particularly friendly, Ian always felt that the real problems were between Colin and Innes, rather than with Jim. Innes was undoubtedly the quicker driver but Colin saw much more potential in Jim, who was also more of a team player, a highly rated quality at Lotus. Jim had now been racing for Lotus for two seasons and in Chapman's mind he was the better driver. Colin also had to select drivers who would get on well together. Jim was definitely not averse to having fun, and there is a great deal of pictorial evidence of this side of his character, but he was a quieter and more serious individual who put his duties first. That made it harder for him to gel with Innes.

News of Jim's ability was spreading and his unassuming demeanour and softly spoken Scots accent endeared him to the British public. His sister Betty remembers travelling with Jim one day about this time. Jim noticed that people were beginning to stare and asked Betty what they were looking at. It was him. He simply had no idea that people would find him interesting just for driving a car quickly. Indeed, Colin later said that if Jim could have his way, 'at the end of each race he would creep away into obscurity until the next one. He was not interested in the glamour.'

Jim had to wait until December for his next win; then he won three more grands prix, all minor events in South Africa.

For the 1962 World Championship Jim was partnered by Taylor, his Formula Junior team-mate from 1960. They started the year with the non-championship grands prix and the Lotus 24 with Coventry Climax V8 engines, but it was soon replaced by the Lotus 25. This car revolutionised F1 design and set the standards for the future. It abandoned the space-frame construction that Lotus had developed in the fifties and replaced it with a monocoque in which the panniers that held the two fuel tanks on either side of the driver were integral to the chassis, which was fitted at the front to the suspension and at the back to the engine. There was another fuel tank behind the driver. This design was more aerodynamic and had the advantage of ensuring that the chassis consisted mostly of fuel tank, minimising the weight of the car while maximising its power.

The drivers, however, had to learn how to get the best out of this new design. According to Jim, 'One of the problems at first with the Lotus 25 was the very reclined seating position, which made visibility difficult, particularly on sharp corners.' He said it 'required some time to become accustomed to. But once I had mastered the new position, I wondered how I had ever driven a racing car any other way.'

The 24 had initially been intended to be the main car for 1962 and, although it was sidelined quite late in the process, it was actually a minor success. On its first appearance, at the Brussels Grand Prix, Jim qualified on pole but dropped out of the race with gearbox problems. He then won the Lombank Trophy at Snetterton and the Aintree 200 and almost won the *Daily Express* Trophy at Silverstone. He should really have won it, having led from the start almost until the finish, but going into the final lap he was ahead of Graham Hill when he got caught up with Masten Gregory, who was running a lap behind. Hill overtook Jim on the line.

The Lotus 25 made its first outing during the Dutch Grand Prix at Zandvoort on 20 May, making the 24 obsolete as far as FI was concerned, although Taylor still had to make do with it. Despite being only third on the grid, Jim took the lead from the start, but trouble with the clutch forced him into the pits. He rejoined but ended up in ninth, an ignominious ten laps behind Graham Hill's winning B.R.M. Taylor finished second.

Jim's next race was the 1,000KM at the Nürburgring in the Lotus 23 sportscar. This car was entered by Essex Racing but the entry was really a Team Lotus enterprise; Mike Costin was in charge of the cars and Taylor was the second driver. This was Dance's first opportunity to work with Jim at a race meeting. He remembers that when the car left Lotus Developments it was not actually in a condition to be driven, let alone raced. In fact, it took more than a day's work to get it race-worthy.

Compared with many of its rivals, the Lotus was quite a small car with only a 1,500cc engine, but it had enough horsepower to make it a serious contender. The race started in very wet conditions and Jim was soon able

'One of the problems with the Lotus 25 was the very reclined seating position, which made visibility difficult. Once I had mastered it, I wondered how I had ever driven any other way.' — Jim Clark

to take the lead from McLaren. The conditions made life difficult for the larger-engined cars and Jim was able to open out almost thirty seconds on the first lap. As Bob recalls, with some emotion in his voice, 'That little Lotus just ran away from the field.'

By the seventh lap Jim had lapped almost half of the field, but then two things began to work against him. The circuit started to dry out, enabling the more powerful cars to increase their speeds, and a cracked manifold was allowing carbon monoxide to seep into the cockpit, which inevitably made Jim drowsy. Eventually he went off the circuit at Hocheichen, after almost two hours in the lead.

Despite crashing out, Jim's accomplishment immediately made him the pre-race favourite for the Index of Performance in the Le Mans 24 Hours,

Previous pages: The West
Essex Car Club dinner
dance in November 1961.
It has a Scottish flavour
with Jim in full regalia,
even if he is wearing a
tartan tammy. Behind
him are Ron Flockhart,
and, slightly less well-
dressed, Graham Hill,
Peter Jopp and John
Cooper.

for which he was entered in the same car. However, he was not to run there. The Lotus 23 was rejected by the French scrutineers and none of the amendments that Costin made met their requirements. Le Mans was the race in which Jim had first really made his mark but he was never to run there again because Colin was becoming more and more disenchanted with the organisers and their complicated rulebook and their unfriendly interpretations of that rulebook – at least, that was how he saw it.

Next up was the Monaco Grand Prix. Again Taylor had to make do with a Lotus 24. After a number of frustrating qualifying sessions Jim managed to come out on top with a lap of 1 minute 35 seconds, just four tenths faster than Graham Hill managed in the B.R.M.

The start of the race was almost disastrous: Mairesse, driving a Ferrari, shot into the lead from the second row. He collided with Jim's Lotus and was moving too fast and lost it at the Gasworks hairpin. It was all that Jim could do to avoid trouble and he dropped to sixth place. By lap twenty-five, however, he had raced through the field into second place with only Hill to catch. Sadly he got caught up with backmarkers and began to have problems with his clutch before dropping out on the fifty-second lap.

Although it was a disappointing result, the Lotus 25 was beginning to show its potential, having qualified on pole and set the fastest lap. It had been quite a gamble for Chapman and he had taken a risk with his company's future but it seemed to be paying off.

Two weeks after Monaco came the Belgian Grand Prix at Spa. Jim's practice was disastrous: the camshaft broke and his engine was sent off for repair. It wasn't back in time for second practice so he took Taylor's Lotus 24 and qualified in the middle of the fifth row with a lap of 4 minutes 4.9 seconds, almost eight seconds slower than Hill was on pole in his B.R.M.

His engine turned up after practice and the Lotus mechanics had to spend their Saturday night fitting it to his car. Taylor's car had also had gearbox problems and the mechanics had to create a new one for him by combining the best parts from two broken ones.

The long nine-mile laps gave Jim plenty of time to work his way though the pack from twelfth on the grid. The power and agility of his Lotus were such that he climbed eight places during the first lap alone. It was not long before the only cars still ahead of him were those that had started on the front row and he was close enough to be within striking distance of Hill, who was leading the race.

By lap three he had dropped back a place and he continued to sit there while the first five cars lapped the circuit in close order. On lap eight he began to move through this group and he took the lead on the following lap. By lap ten he was leading from his team-mate, who began to hold up

the other cars to allow Jim to pull away. Jim was able cruise around the circuit for the 25's first grand prix win.

Meanwhile, the main interest was a fight between Taylor and Mairesse, who passed and repassed each other until lap twenty-six, when they collided. The Lotus went into a ditch and the Ferrari turned over and caught fire. Luckily neither was badly hurt, although Mairesse was slightly burned.

Lotus took part in the Reims Grand Prix at the beginning of July, a non-championship event. Jim qualified on pole position but in the race he came into the pits on lap five with a crack in the cooling system and swapped his car for Peter Arundell's Lotus B.R.M. – an eventuality that was still fairly common outside the world championship – but it was to no avail and Jim dropped out on the thirty-seventh lap after running out of fuel.

The French Grand Prix was at Rouen the following week. A new Lotus 25 was available for Jim and Taylor drove the original 25. Jim managed to qualify on the front of the grid but it was not to be his race. He was never really happy with the car and, although he took the lead briefly on lap

The 1962 International Trophy race at Silverstone. From the start Jim in the Lotus 24 was able to open a big lead from American driver Richie Ginther in the B.R.M.

Jim at the wheel of the Lotus 23 at the 1962 Nürburgring 1,000KM race. Although it left the factory in poor racing condition, Jim was able to run away from the field before retiring suffering from carbon monoxide poisoning.

thirty, and he had to withdraw from the race with steering problems after just four laps out front.

The British Grand Prix was held at Aintree and Jim kept up his qualifying performance, starting from the front. Once the race started, it was the same again. He gently eased away from the field, eventually winning from Surtees' Lola by about fifty seconds. Only two other drivers, McLaren and Graham Hill, were on the same lap. The British Grand Prix was to be one of Jim's 'go to' races: he failed to win it only three times out of eight attempts. More important, this was his second win in the season, which left him in a good position for the drivers' world championship, although Hill was emerging as his main rival, having won and finished in the minor points as well, which Jim had not.

Unfortunately Jim was to remedy that 'fault' during the German Grand Prix at the Nürburgring. He qualified third but had a terrible start. The race was run in wet conditions and Jim, struggling with damp goggles that kept misting up, forgot to switch on his fuel pump. The flag came down and the field left the starting grid, leaving Jim sitting in his Lotus 25 waiting for his carburettors to fill with fuel. He eventually got going and began to demonstrate that he and the 25 were an ominous combination. Like Spa, the long Nürburgring circuit, although demanding, is a delight for fast, powerful cars and Jim quickly began to pick off the 'minnows' in the pack. By the time he finished the fourteen miles of the first lap he had already overtaken seventeen of the twenty-five cars that had been ahead of him.

The cars were running comparatively slowly because of the bad conditions. Gurney was leading but was lapping almost two minutes slower than his fastest qualifying lap had been. Jim eventually made it into fourth place but could get no farther and Hill managed to overtake Gurney and hold onto the lead despite having to drive 'around' his fire extinguisher, which had come loose and was rolling around inside his cockpit. For Jim, it was a fantastic drive from near-last to fourth in terrible conditions on one of the world's most dangerous circuits.

The next grand prix was at Monza, Jim's first return to Italy since the previous year's disaster. The banked sections of the track were not being used this time; instead the race was to run on the road circuit. Both drivers had Lotus 25s and the team took a 24 as a spare. Jim had terrible problems with gearboxes and ended up using Taylor's Lotus to take pole for the race, only three thousandths of a second faster than Hill. In the race itself, Hill flashed past Jim soon after the start and things got worse from there. He was in the pits on lap three with gearbox problems and out of the race by lap thirteen as they worsened. Even worse, Hill had led the race from start to finish to record yet another victory. With all the European races over, Jim now had to win in the United States if he was to have any hope of becoming world champion this year.

He did not let the pressure get to him. On the first day of practice at Watkins Glen he recorded the fastest time of 1 minute 15.8 seconds. Final qualifying was marred by rain and no one was able to better his Friday times. In fact, many drivers had problems keeping their cars on the track, but Jim and Graham were the most competitive, setting identical fastest times.

When the race started, Hill moved from third on the grid into second place and he and Jim began to pull away from the rest of the field. On the twelfth lap Hill took advantage of the need to lap backmarkers and seized the lead from Jim. With the championship on the line, Jim was forced to show his mettle and gradually cranked up the pressure on Hill's B.R.M. before passing him on the nineteenth lap. That was it for the race. Hill never got the lead back but Jim had to keep up the pace to stay in front. His winning gap was a little over nine seconds – comfortable but with no margin for error.

The year's final grand prix, in South Africa, was to be held on 29 December after what must have seemed an intolerable gap of about ten weeks. Before this, however, there was plenty of other racing to be done: Jim competed unsuccessfully in the 1,000KM of Paris in an Aston Martin DB4 with Whitmore. There was a non-championship grand prix in Mexico City in early November, during which Ricardo Rodriguez was killed in Rob Walker's privately entered Lotus. As well as reminding people of the dangers of motorsport, this race epitomised the simpler and more sporting nature of F1 in the sixties: Jim's Lotus 25 was push-started and he was disqualified for it on lap eleven. Taylor was called in and allowed to take over his car, which he drove to victory. Swapping cars was an old practice that had been outlawed in the championship but it could still work to Jim's advantage away from the main series.

Then there were two minor F1 races, in which Jim came first (the Rand Grand Prix at Kyalami in South Africa) and second (the Natal Grand Prix, also in South Africa). Just as in their Formula Junior days, Taylor came second and first, securing two one-two finishes for the team.

Finally, it was time for the final championship grand prix, on South Africa's East London circuit by the shores of the Indian Ocean, on narrow public roads that were closed for the race. Colin took three cars in the hope of having two ready for the race – it would have been impossible to

The French GP at Rouen, 1962. Jim is on the right-hand side of the grid. His Lotus 25 retired on the 33rd lap with suspension failure.

fly out parts at the last minute. Initial qualifying did not go well; the new 25 with a fuel injection system kept cutting out and Taylor's car was unable to run. On the final two days of practice Jim got quicker and quicker, as did Hill, and on race day the championship rivals occupied the front row of the grid with Jim, as had become usual, just ahead of Graham.

Jim had to win this race to take the crown, towards which only a driver's five best results counted. He had won as many races as Hill but had failed to finish more times, which gave Graham an edge over him. Jim gave it his all, opening up a lead of about a second a lap over the first few

laps. By about the halfway stage things were looking good. Jim had a lead of almost thirty seconds and it seemed that there was nothing Hill could do about it.

On lap sixty-one smoke began to stream from Jim's engine and he was soon out of the race, leaving Hill to become world champion.

Investigation of Jim's Lotus later showed that a bolt had dropped off the crank case and so had never been fitted. Before the race, Colin had been distracted by a perceived need to reduce the Lotus's weight because B.R.M. had been putting it around that it was going to run a lighter car in

Jim leads the field at Aintree in 1962 on his way to his first win in the British GP.

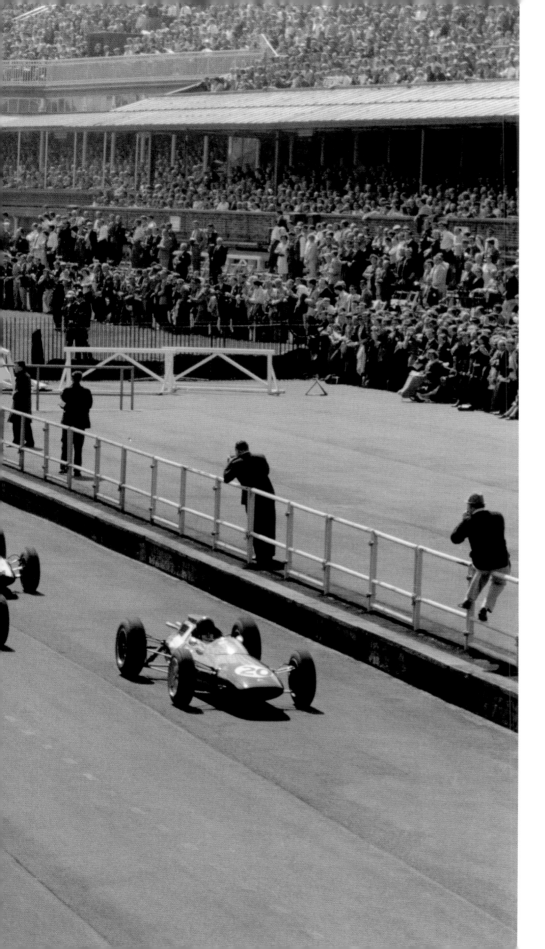

The start of the 1962 British GP at Aintree with Jim making a characteristic push from the off. Aintree developed a motor racing circuit in the 1950s to boost the income required to manage the National Hunt race course.

South Africa. It was an understandable mistake given the circumstances and the pressure that everyone faced, but it was an extremely costly one. The team had had the main prize in its sights, but the world championship was ultimately decided by a lack of attention to detail in the construction of Jim's Lotus 25.

When Jim returned to Britain he was photographed smiling as he went through Heathrow Airport. He knew he had given it his best shot. Lotus had run a revolutionary car that had ended 1962 more than competitive: it was the best car. It was only to be expected that there would be teething problems and if these could be put right, 1963 was looking good.

Opposite: Jim gets a first-hand look at the competition – a Ferrari FI Dino 156 car at the German GP in 1962 – with Colin Chapman eagerly looking on. Not something that would happen today.

Above: Jim surrounded by the press and fans at Watkins Glen in 1962.

Waiting for the flag to drop: Jim and Graham Hill are ready to battle it out for the 1962 World Championship in the final race of the season at East London. After opening up a lead of a second a lap Jim was leading Hill by nearly half a minute at half way when his engine failed – a bolt had come loose from the crank case.

Chapter 4
The Years of Victory

AFTER NARROWLY LOSING OUT ON the world championship in the last grand prix of 1962, Jim was about to enter the most successful phase of his career. Every time he had finished a grand prix that year he had either won the race or been close to the winner's laurels. Furthermore, he had shown that the Lotus 25 with its Coventry Climax engine was going to be the leading car for 1963.

Colin Chapman had ambitious plans for Lotus and Jim Clark. He was determined that 1963 was going to be their year in Formula 1 and that Jim would finish the season as champion. Moreover, Colin had been invited to the Indianapolis 500 race in 1962 and had been astonished by an event that was, in F1 terms, ritualistic and anachronistic. It consisted of just over thirty cars powered by front-mounted Offenhauser engines racing around an oval track. Front-engined cars were long dead in Europe but here they were the pinnacle of racing achievement. Every 500 since 1937 had been won by one. If you wanted to win at Indy, that was the way to go. You no more put any other kind of engine in your car than the winning driver would refuse the traditional celebratory glass of milk.

Below: The monocoque construction of the Lotus 25.

Dan Gurney, Jim's great American rival, had suggested that Colin enter a car in the race. After his initial surprise at seeing the race, Colin agreed with him and decided to design a car that would show the Americans what real racing was all about, especially when driven by a racing master: Jim.

Jim did not race in the Tasman Series this year. Instead he stayed in Britain and helped develop the Lotus Cortina sports saloon car, yet another car in which he was to achieve a level of greatness that has probably never been surpassed. He was also involved in developing the Lotus for Indianapolis, which would happen in May.

Gurney had convinced Ford to get involved. They had developed an aluminium v8 Fairline engine, which was to be fitted into a modified Lotus 25, known as the Lotus 29. The wheelbase had to be extended to eight feet, the minimum allowed at Indianapolis. Indy cars also had offset suspension because they were always turning left on a banked circuit, putting a downward and sideways pressure on the suspension. The car would also have six fuel tanks to carry the required fifty gallons of fuel.

So Jim had a very busy diary. The grand prix calendar was typically crowded, with almost thirty races, of which only ten counted towards the world championship and from those a driver could count only his six best finishes. The main contenders would enter every championship event but would otherwise pick and choose where to race. In between all these races, Jim was busy flying back and forth across the Atlantic preparing for Indy.

His first race was at the end of March: the Lombank Trophy at Snetterton, in which he came second. This was the first of five non-championship races in six weeks. Jim won three of them and came third in another, at Aintree. His battery failed at Aintree, losing him a lot of time at the start and he had to take Trevor Taylor's car. Jim carved his way through the field, which he thoroughly enjoyed. He may have finished only third but in the circumstances it was a great achievement.

Then came the opening championship event, in Monaco, billed as the Grand Prix of Europe. Due to the tight and twisty nature of the two-mile circuit, only sixteen entries were guaranteed places on the grid and, of these, five places were allocated to the current champion and the four competing ex-champions. Neither Lotus nor Ferrari had a champion.

Jim qualified on pole with almost his final lap of second practice, with a time of 1 minute 34.3 seconds. Jack Brabham was lucky with the rule about champions being automatically qualified because his engine blew in first practice and he managed only the last place on the grid. For Jim, and no doubt for other drivers, this was good news. Brabham would never do anything dangerous but experience had taught him how to make his car very wide, which made Jim wary of having to overtake him, particularly on a street circuit. As it turned out, Brabham wouldn't have started at all had Colin not been persuaded to lend him the spare works Lotus.

Jim came second in the Lombank Trophy at Snetterton in 1963 in the Lotus 25. This was his first outing of the 1963 season.

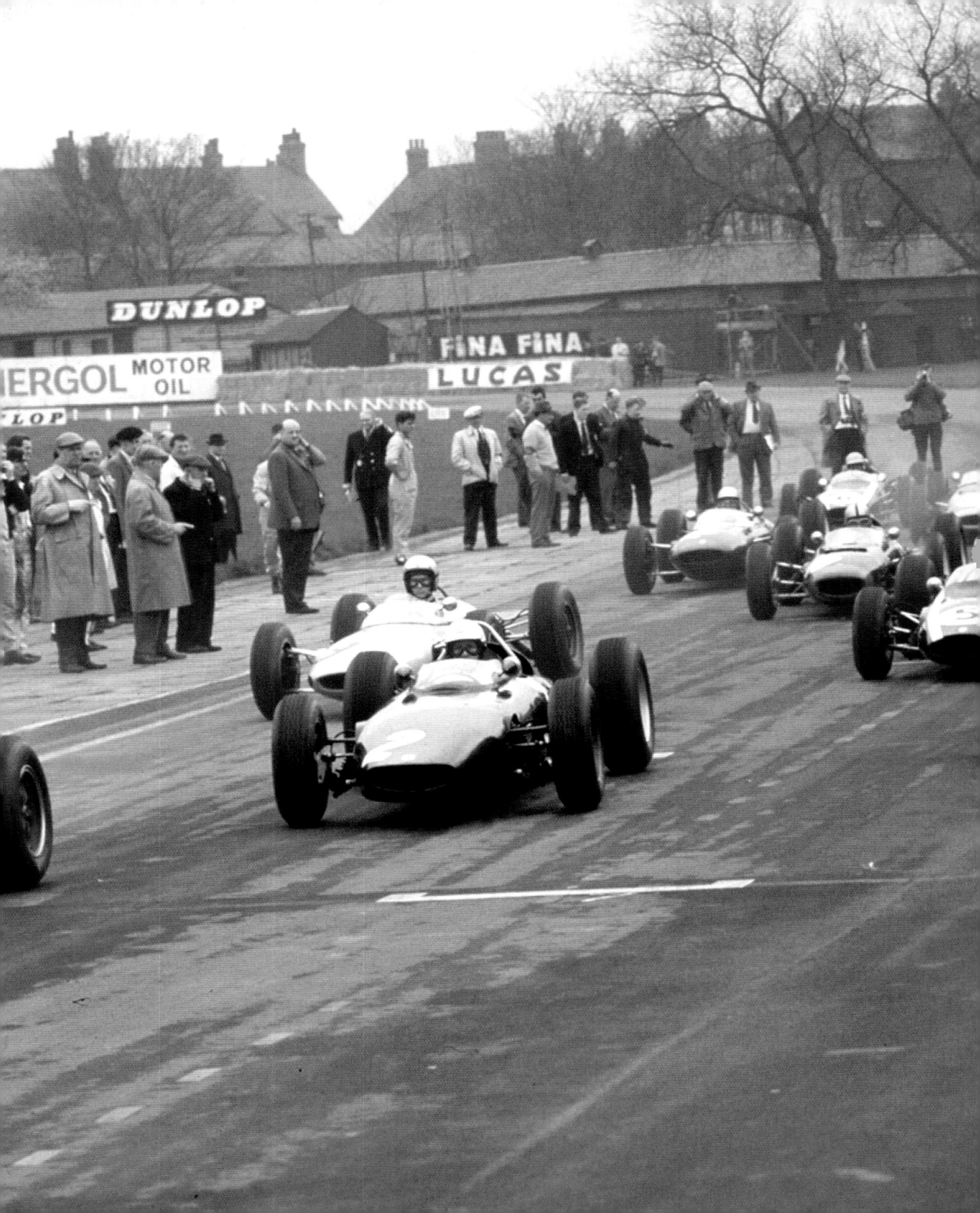
DUNLOP
FINA FINA
LUCAS
ERGOL MOTOR OIL

After a desperate struggle with Graham Hill for the lead over the opening laps, Jim eventually made an overtaking manoeuvre stick on the seventeenth lap and gradually began to open out a commanding lead. It all came unstuck on the seventy-ninth lap, however, when the Lotus gearbox seized with both second and fourth gears engaged. There was nothing Jim could do; his race was run and the season was off to a disappointing start.

The Lotus 29, for the Indy 500, wasn't ready until March. The team first tested it at Snetterton and then, later in March, took it to Kingman, Arizona, for hot-weather testing on a five-mile oval circuit. Then it was back to Indy in April for Jim to pass his learner tests: it made no difference to the Americans that he'd narrowly missed out on the FI championship. FI was no big deal but, just to make sure, they heaped on the pressure.

One other thing had to change; the car's colour scheme. At Indianapolis green was considered an unlucky colour so, to smooth relations with the Americans, Lotus added a yellow stripe to its cars.

Jim had little time to bemoan his Monaco disappointment because the Indy 500 was only four days away. He left Monaco at 4.30 a.m. the next day to go to London to catch a flight to the States. He was arriving rather late for practice, which had been taking place over the previous month: at Indianapolis the race was just the final act, albeit the most important one.

The Indy-style front-engined roadsters may have been anachronisms in FI terms but they were quick and well-designed for driving on oval circuits such as Indy. Jim had to learn new tricks if he was going to shine there: turning left at the end of each straight may sound easy but doing it at speed on heavily banked curves was entirely new to him.

It wasn't the first time an FI driver had competed at Indy; Brabham had been there in 1961 and Alberto Ascari and Giuseppe Farina had driven there for Ferrari, without success. But Clark and Lotus were the most serious European contenders for a long time and they initially got a less-than-friendly reception. Jim's practice laps were undertaken in front of a large audience of officials and drivers who seemed keen to intimidate him as he went about learning the ropes. Maybe they just wanted to see the European who had come second in the FI championship, but it's more likely they were just interested in the latest small-car challenger. It was very different from what Jim was used to.

The circuit itself was not exactly stimulating for a driver who was used to the varying challenges of the European circuits such as Monza, Spa and Monte Carlo, though Jim later said the circuit changes all the time, making it difficult to get it right and therefore not too boring. To win at Indy you had to be good at turning left for 250 laps over 500 miles, which was physically very demanding. It's difficult to maintain a high level of concentration on what is essentially a featureless track. Jim needed to drive in top gear all the time and the difficulty was in finding the braking points.

Previous pages: Jim sits in his Lotus with his arm aloft. The engine had failed to ignite at the start of the BARC race at Aintree in 1963.

Opposite: Graham Hill leads from Jim early in the 1963 Monaco GP.

The first time he drove on the circuit, his car was set up for Watkins Glen, which was more typical of a grand prix circuit. Despite this, Jim drove through the bends faster than any Indy car had done so far.

The management of the race is totally different from that of a grand prix. Instead of two days before the race, the whole of May is given over to practice and qualifying. The organisers are past masters at marketing; as race day gets closer, the whole of Indianapolis seems to become a circus. For Jim, this would be a major distraction, but racing in Europe the weekend before probably helped to insulate him from the hullabaloo.

Bob Dance went out to Indy in 1965 for Lotus. From his British perspective, he describes Indy as a way of life for the month of May. The track opened up for qualifying on the first of the month and the race was held on Memorial Day at the end of the month. By and large the mechanics were put up in cheap but good accommodation, although it was not a lot better for the Lotus drivers. In 1963 Jim shared a room with Colin – and two others slept on the floor. Virtually everything was spent on the circuit and everyone ate in the canteen on Gasoline Alley. In Europe the drivers' wives and girlfriends went to the circuits and helped out with timing, but they were completely absent from Indy: they were just not allowed. Nothing was to distract the teams from preparing for the race.

Bob had the feeling that the Americans didn't 'really get the limeys with their Beatle haircuts'. No serious competitor would waste time in another race the week before – and certainly not on another continent. However, Colin used his time at Indy carefully, taking advantage of the cool mornings and evenings to get the most out of the cars, drivers and mechanics.

In the race itself, Jim started slowly. It had a rolling start, which was a novelty to him, and being tightly surrounded by a large field of cars throughout the race was a very different experience from running in a grand prix, where he'd be constantly manoeuvring past slower cars. On the oval circuit there was absolutely no time to switch off and relax.

Parnelli Jones, driving a Watson-Offenhauser for Aggie Agajanian, was Jim's great rival. Jim took the lead for a while when Jones pitted for the first time and he hoped that once all the pitstops were out of the way he would be in the lead with Jones having to pass him. It could have worked but the inevitable accidents during the race worked out in Jones' favour: he was able to take his second and third stops under the cautionary yellow lights, while the field was running slowly, giving him time to get in and out.

The real controversy happened after the final pitstops when Parnelli Jones' car began to leak oil. In the pre-race briefing everyone had been told that, for safety reasons, an oil leak would lead to automatic disqualification. The risk of spinning is much greater on an oval track, especially if it's oily. However, Agajanian persuaded Harlan Fengler, clerk of the course, to delay his decision. By the time Fengler was ready to rule, the leak had stopped.

Back in Scotland, Jim's father and sister Betty had been listening to the race on a radio linked up to the Lotus pits at Indy. Jim's mother never got any pleasure out of his racing and couldn't bear to listen or watch. She just wanted to know that he was safe and how he had done.

Coming second was a great achievement and Jim won the prize for being the best rookie, but it was not enough. To him, rules were rules and it just wasn't cricket to have them set aide for the home team. He was so annoyed that he persuaded Colin to let him race at two more oval circuits that year, at Milwaukee and Trenton. Both were Indy-style races run over 250 miles. Jim won the first with a lap record and retired at Trenton while leading the race. Ironically it was an oil leak that caused him to drop out.

Back in Europe after their glorious failure at Indy, Jim and Colin had a world championship to win. This was their bread and butter. The next race was the Belgian Grand Prix at Spa on 9 June. Jim could qualify only eighth, with Graham Hill in the B.R.M. on pole position. In damp conditions Jim made a tremendous start, shooting into the lead. He was initially pursued by Hill and Gurney but they dropped back, leaving Bruce McLaren as the main challenger. At the end of the race McLaren was the only finisher on the same lap as Jim, almost five minutes behind him.

'I found that on the fast corners on the back of the circuit, I could set the car up on one big drift and just jam my foot on the throttle.' — Jim Clark

The third grand prix of the season was the Dutch, held at Zandvoort on 23 June. Jim qualified first and led from the start, setting a blistering pace. The only other noteworthy occurrence was that Gurney dropped to last place at the start and came through the field to finish second. Such was Jim's dominance that he had lapped Gurney at the halfway point, on lap forty, and he held this to finish a lap ahead of him.

The French Grand Prix was held at Reims a week later. First practice was on the Wednesday evening, a little over seventy-two hours after the end of the previous race. The Lotus 25 was slower on the straights than the B.R.Ms and Ferraris but Jim 'found that on the fast corners on the back of the circuit, I could set the car up on one big drift and just jam my foot on the throttle'. He took pole. Yet again Jim led from start to finish, although his engine began to develop problems and it was only thanks to rain later in the race, which slowed the cars, that he was able to stay out in front, despite aquaplaning on near-bald tyres. He still finished more than a minute ahead of his nearest rival, Tony Maggs in a Cooper Climax.

After this, the drivers and teams had three weeks to prepare for the British Grand Prix at Silverstone on 20 July. As had become normal, Jim qualified on pole – but things did not go according to plan in the race. He dropped to a lowly fifth place during the first lap, but by lap four he had crept back to his accustomed position and started opening out a healthy lead. For the spectators, the race for the lead was unexciting, with Jim finishing over twenty-five seconds ahead of John Surtees, his nearest rival, even though he coasted in the closing laps to conserve fuel. Only Surtees and Hill, out of thirteen finishers, managed to finish on the same lap.

Immediately after his slowing-down lap, Jim dived into the pits instead of continuing to the finishing line as normal. A few minutes later a tractor appeared from the pitlane, pulling a trailer with Jim's Lotus on the back alongside Jim, Colin and a bagpiper playing *Scotland the Brave*. Although very respectful of other nations, Jim was as passionate about his nationality as any other Scot and victory in the British Grand Prix provided a good occasion to show off his patriotism. Colin was more of a natural showman than Jim, but they probably concocted the celebration together.

The German Grand Prix was held two weeks later at the Nürburgring. Jim qualified on pole yet again. He had raced with the same car and engine the week before at Solitude, Germany, so Lotus fitted a new Climax v8 and zf gearbox. There was no reverse gear, to minimise selection problems. Jim shot into the lead of the race but was almost immediately overhauled. His new engine was misfiring and he struggled to keep it going. Despite this, he managed to keep with Surtees, who was leading in a Ferrari. With only two of the fifteen fourteen-mile laps remaining he was still only twenty seconds adrift but he had to ease off. In the circumstances, second place was a great achievement and it left him needing only a good finish at Monza to clinch the championship with three races to spare.

It had been planned that the banked sections of the Monza track would be used for the Italian Grand Prix, but after an accident in practice the Italian police decided it was too great a risk to spectator safety. They had to use the road circuit instead. This was something of a relief to most of the drivers, for Monza had a history of serious accidents on the banked curves.

Jim started practice well but a lack of power restricted him to third on the grid. The mechanics had to replace his engine for the race. Because Jim was worried about the engine, his strategy was as usual to start fast and hope to be able to slipstream the leading cars. Surtees made a dreadful start from pole and Jim got past, bringing him behind Hill. By the fourth lap Surtees was in the lead and Hill had dropped back.

Lap after lap Jim kept his car close to Surtees' Ferrari, sometimes trying to overtake but always lacking the power to get past and having to drop back into the slipstream. But after sixteen laps Jim entered the start-finish straight out front, Surtees' car trailing white smoke from a blown engine.

Jim speaking to fellow Lotus driver Peter Arundell during practice for the French GP in 1963. Although he took part in practice Arundell drove in the Formula Junior race.

Jim is hidden by a fast-moving starter as
the French GP gets under way at Reims.
Graham Hill is in the middle in the B.R.M.
with Dan Gurney in the Brabham on
the right.

Jim being interviewed by journalists during the French GP weekend at Reims in 1963.

Now that Clark couldn't slipstream the Ferrari, Hill and Gurney quickly caught up with him. The three had a titanic struggle for the lead, which changed hands a number of times over the next thirty laps before Hill's B.R.M. dropped out with clutch trouble. Gurney and Clark then shared the lead for a while before Gurney retired on the sixty-fifth lap, leaving Jim to cruise to victory with only one other car on the same lap.

It was his toughest race of the season and, with the title secured, would have been a sweet feeling if only the Italian police hadn't been there. They were still investigating the death of Von Trips in 1961 and Jim was able to leave the country only once he had the details of a lawyer to represent him.

Lotus was now the FI constructor's champion. For Colin, this was a vindication, showing that his cars were reliable. Only once all year had Jim failed to finish – which was noticed by advertisers and potential buyers.

So there was no pressure on Lotus for Watkins Glen in October. Only honour (and, of course, prize money) was at stake. Jim qualified second

A portrait of Jim during the 1963 British GP weekend at Silverstone.

Below: Jim's Lotus 25 on a trailer being towed by a tractor around Silverstone after winning the 1963 British GP. According to the *Motorsport* report of the race this was entirely unexpected and seems to have been planned by Colin Chapman and Jim as a novel means of celebrating.

Previous pages: Jim holds the British GP trophy aloft at Silverstone in 1963. This was his fourth win of the season and he was well on the way to winning the championship.

Above: Jim with John Surtees (left) at the Nürburgring, 1963.

but had a bad start. The battery played up and the last car had done a lap before he got going. Jim cut through the field to finish third, a lap down.

At the end of October Mexico held its first championship event on a three-mile-long circuit in Mexico City. Jim qualified on pole, almost two seconds faster than anyone else. Jim won the race in typical style, leading from start to finish and ending with only two other cars, those of Brabham (a Brabham car) and Ginther, on the same lap.

The 1963 South African Grand Prix was rather devalued. With the championship having been decided at Monza, South Africa seemed a long way for some of the teams to go over the Christmas holiday. Only five works teams went, plus a Rob Walker car, the rest of the entry being local drivers. Jim qualified on pole position alongside Gurney and Brabham.

Jim and Brabham started well but Jim managed to hold his position. Once team-mate Taylor came through into second place, he was able to hold Brabham and Gurney for a while, allowing Jim to open up a significant gap. Taylor wasn't fast enough to remain in second and

Brabham spun off. Jim retained his lead until the end, taking his seventh win of the season, more than any other driver had achieved before.

After the season, Jim was asked about his skills and explained them thus: 'I think the most important thing in motor racing is concentration. If I want to go faster, I don't *drive* any faster; I just concentrate harder.'

Jim's championship excited Scotland – and Berwickshire in particular. The Berwick Motor Club announced that it would hold a function in his honour. The day after he returned, Jim toured in an open-topped bus. One of his sisters remembers that he was unsure what he should wear and she had to persuade him to wear his Lotus overalls. On the bus with Jim and some family members were some players from the local pipe band.

They were led by a police car and went though Foulden, Ayton, Reston, Edrom, Allanton and Chirnside, all local villages in which Jim was well known. Then, in a ceremony in Chirnside, Jim was given an inscribed

'I'd follow Jim into a corner thinking, "By God, he's going to go off at that speed," then he'd just somehow gather it all together. I've no idea how he did it; it was like magic.'
— Trevor Taylor

shepherd's crook. He made a speech, thanking his family, Ian and the late Jock McBain for their support and encouragement of his career.

For 1964, Lotus developed a new version of the 25, known as the Lotus 33, with revised suspension and a simplified and stronger monocoque. The Cosworth Climax engine was updated to produce 200B.H.P. The 33 wasn't the radical departure that the 25 had been and should have been up to speed much quicker but this would prove to be a year of frustration in FI.

There were other changes, too. Jim had a new team-mate in Peter Arundell. Taylor had just had too many crashes for Colin's liking. According to Dance, many of them were not really Taylor's fault, but he had an unhappy knack of getting himself into situations in which accidents happen. Jim, of course, was the exact opposite; his smooth driving style and keen racing brain kept him out of trouble. Taylor once said of Clark: 'I'd follow him into a corner thinking, "By God, he's going to go off at that speed," then he'd just somehow gather it all together . . . I've no idea how he did it; it was like magic.'

Arundell felt he could beat Jim if he had the same car with the same support. This turned out not really to be the case but it did ensure that there was no complacency within the team.

World champion at last. Having just
clinched his first world championship
winning the Italian GP at Monza Jim,
smothered in the victor's laurel wreath,
drives the Lotus 25 round the circuit
with Colin Chapman holding the trophy
out to the applauding crowds.

Wheelspin at the start of the 1963 South
African Grand Prix. Jim is on the left with
Jack Brabham beside him and Dan Gurney
on the right.

Jim at the wheel of a car from a gentler age of motoring. He poses for the press in a Model T Ford at a Scottish Motor show, c.1963.

Below: Jim and Andrew Cowan, a successful rally driver from the 1960s, a friend of Jim's from his early days of racing and the first winner of a shield presented by Jim to the Berwick and District Motor Club in 1963.

Opposite: Jim Clark Day. Jim stands on the back of a decorated flat-bed lorry the week after he had clinched his second world championship to be presented with a wrought iron sign to hang outside his farm.

Returning from South Africa at the start of 1963. Jim was putting on a brave face for the press waiting at Heathrow. He had just narrowly missed winning the world championship, losing to Graham Hill at East London at the end of December.

Lotus had also been working with Ford on a Cortina for touring car races, on which Jim worked hard during 1964 with his mechanic Dance.

Bob recalls that Jim absolutely loved racing the Cortina, in which he had a lot of fun and demonstrated his total command of the vehicle. On some bends he would drive on three or even two wheels. You couldn't do

that in an FI car. In many ways, racing the Cortina was similar to the racing with which Jim had started his career; the races were shorter than grands prix but he was still pitted against high-quality fields and in a car prepared by a professional team.

There were about ten races in the 1964 British Saloon Car Championship, of which Jim would win seven in the Cortina. Some races clashed with FI events and Lotus had to bring in other drivers for them.

Jim also drove the Cortina in longer events at Sebring, Florida. On two consecutive days, 22 and 23 March, he entered the 250KM race and then the twelve-hour race, winning the first and coming second in the other.

Jim opening the Scottish Motor Show from the stand of Ecurie Ecosse, the main rivals of the Border Reivers.

Jim driving N°70 at Snetterton in the 1964 British Saloon Car Championship. The Lotus Cortina was probably the car Jim enjoyed racing the most with his distinctive three-wheeled style of cornering.

His first grand prix of the year was at Snetterton in March. He raced a modified Lotus 25 and, in the heavy rain that shortened the race to only 35 laps, never really got going. His start was poor and his tyres had no grip on the wet surface. Arundell was outperforming Jim until he spun out of the race, which was eventually won by Innes Ireland with Jim fourth.

As usual, the first championship grand prix was in Monaco in May. Jim had crashed the 33 during the Aintree Gold Cup, so was back in a 25 for this race. It was a modified 25B, with the lower suspension of the 33 and smaller Dunlop tyres. He missed first practice on the Thursday because he was driving in practice at Indianapolis, preparing for the Indy 500 later in the month. On the Friday, showing no signs of jetlag, he quickly got into the rhythm of driving, setting his pole position time in the first of his two qualifying sessions. Brabham qualified alongside him, one tenth of a second slower.

Jim made a tremendous start and began easing away, slowly but steadily, from his pursuers, who were desperately trying to keep him in sight. His rear anti-roll bar hung loose from the twenty-third lap, but this was just another opportunity for him to demonstrate his mastery of the car: he merely altered his driving style and continued on his merry way. A pitstop to remove the bar dropped him back to third but with only four laps to go he had retire with low oil. He was classified fourth, but nonetheless it was a disappointing end to what had started so well.

The Dutch Grand Prix was held the week before the Indy 500 and, as in the previous year, Lotus refused to allow its plans to race in America to get in the way of the FI championship. Both cars were the same as at Monaco, although Arundell's had been brought more into line with the 33 design and the anti-roll bars had been redesigned to keep them secure.

Jim was a keen cricket player. He is in the background of this shot while his great friend John Whitmore keeps wicket in a charity cricket match.

Practice and qualifying went well, with Jim second on the grid behind Gurney's Brabham. In effect, Jim won the race in the first bend, where he outbraked Gurney and held off Hill's attempts to go around the outside. After that he gradually pulled away from the field, dropping his pursuers one by one with his precise, easy driving style. By the end, only Surtees was on the same lap and he was more than fifty seconds adrift. All in all this was a smooth performance. Jim comfortably broke his lap record from the previous year and it seemed he had a good chance of defending his title.

Next up was the Indy 500. Lotus and Ford had been developing a car that had been through intensive testing over the winter and spring. Unlike Brabham, who had missed most of the practice at Zandvoort because he still had to qualify at Indy, Lotus had made sure that its drivers had qualified earlier in May, before the Monaco Grand Prix.

The Lotus was designated a 34 and was a modified 29 with a new Ford engine; it was really a modified Offenhauser engine designed to fit the chassis. But Colin made one big mistake: tyre choice. It was normal to use Firestone tyres at Indy but Colin was more familiar with Dunlop, the universal choice in FI and probably a more versatile and better tyre. But the heavy banking, near-continuous left-hand turns and more demanding road surface made the Dunlop risky.

All was well in qualifying; the Lotus cars were way ahead of their rivals but, afterwards, in testing with full tanks, the tyres suffered undue amounts of wear. Dunlop produced a slightly different version for the race but it, too, proved inadequate.

Jim ran in the lead for about seven laps but then the tread came off one his rear tyres, breaking his suspension and throwing him into the wall. Colin decided that his efforts were over for that year and called Gurney in to retire. In his mind, it was just too dangerous to continue. It was a great disappointment for Lotus but made the team realise that it had to get serious to win at Indy. The following year Jim and Colin would have a new, more focused approach to the project.

Jim's next race was the grand prix at Spa in Belgium. He was still running a modified Lotus 25, though in practice he used both the 25 and the 33. Qualifying did not go well. On the Friday evening, his car probably spent more time in the hands of the mechanics, who were trying to tweak more power out of it, than it did out on the track. In the second and final

Opposite: Cornering the Lotus 32 at the non-championship race at the Circuit de Pau, 1964.

Above: Jim waits for confirmation of lap times, Monaco GP weekend, 1964.

Overleaf: Two photographs of the start of the 1964 Monaco GP. Jim is on the right with Jack Brabham beside him. Graham Hill challenges through the middle as the flag drops.

Jim races past the harbour, leading the 1964 Monaco GP. Despite retiring just before the end he was classified as coming 4th.

practice he even started one lap in the 33 but finished it in a 25 – Lotus's off-circuit base was near the track and Jim really wanted the 25, which was not available in the pits when he went out, so he drove off-track to get it.

In these circumstances he could qualify on only the third row of the grid. Gurney led the way in the race. Jim got up to third by the second lap, but was nowhere near the pace of Gurney's Brabham. Yet again he demonstrated his ability to fight for position with a car that was not up to standard. It held him in good stead as the race began to wind down. There was even time for a quick pitstop, which dropped him to fourth.

Then McLaren, in third, started running low on petrol and there was none in his pit. Hill's car, in second, developed a fuel system problem.

And Gurney ran out of petrol on the final lap, allowing Jim into the lead and onto the chequered flag, which had been waved in error for Ginther in the B.R.M. Jim didn't initially know he'd won. Then he, too, ran out of petrol on his slowing-down lap and had to be rescued by Arundell.

It is difficult to know what Jim and Lotus could have taken from this race that they didn't know already. Jim could drive very fast and compete. The new car was unready but motor racing, especially as carried out by Colin, is about developing better and faster cars and that means dealing

Previous page: Dan Gurney and Jim chat on the circuit after the end of the 1964 Belgian GP. Jim had just run out of fuel on his slowing down lap and hadn't yet realised that he had won the race despite passing Dan, who had been leading, and who had also had run out of fuel.

This page: Jim in the Lotus 25 on his way to winning the 1964 Belgian GP at Spa-Francorchamps.

with teething problems. They must have wondered how the rest of the season was going to pan out.

The French Grand Prix was held at Rouen at the end of June. Lotus still hadn't settled the conundrum of which cars to run. Arundell had a 25B and Jim again had the choice of two. Practice and qualifying were held on Thursday and Friday and Jim ran both cars, doing well with both but getting his pole position in the 33. He decided to race the 25B.

The race had a very familiar Jim Clark pattern: he shot into an early lead with only Gurney staying with him in the early stages. Just when it looked cut and dried, and he had a healthy lead over Gurney, one of the engine pistons went and that was that. Gurney took his first grand prix victory, which seemed fitting after his disappointment at Spa.

This year it was Britain's turn to host the Grand Prix of Europe, which was held at Brands Hatch; it was the circuit's first grand prix. Brands Hatch has lots of twists and hills. It is not a high-speed circuit but it is very demanding and draining for the drivers.

Jim strolling along the track with Graham Hill at the Formula 2 GP at Reims in 1964.

Arundell was out following an accident at Reims and his place was taken by Mike Spence in a 25B. Jim ran a 33 in practice but then swapped cars with Spence. In the Thursday practice he was lying third but late in the Friday session he seized pole with a time of 1 minute 38.1 seconds, 0.2 seconds faster than Hill.

For the race itself Jim went back to the 25B and led from the start, closely pursued by Hill. Gurney had been up there at the start but had to pit for eight laps with electrical problems so the race was all about Clark and Hill. Jim was unable to open out any real lead except when lapping backmarkers. Hill tried hard but could not find a way past and Jim held on with less than a three-second lead over eighty laps to win. It was his and Lotus's last good day of the season, although they couldn't know it. With three grand prix wins Jim was in a good position to retain his title but he still needed to finish well in at least some of the upcoming grands prix.

For the German Grand Prix, Lotus ran a third car driven by German Gerhard Mitter. Jim and Spence drove the other two. Mitter didn't even get into a car until the end of final practice, when Colin was happy with Jim's qualifying time and the ability of the Lotus 33 to run in the race. Jim was driving a 33 for the first time in a championship race, no doubt buoyed after winning the South German Grand Prix in one at Solitude. Although he qualified well, in second, and started well – leading the race during the first lap – he soon developed engine problems and dropped back through the field. He retired on the eighth lap. Surtees took over the lead and went on to win in his fast-improving Ferrari.

The Austrian Grand Prix formed part of the championship for the first time in 1964. The circuit was on a military airfield at Zeltweg. Spence was still with Lotus, driving the 33 that Jim had used at Solitude while Jim had one with a few more refinements. Jim qualified third but had a bad race start, having trouble engaging first gear on the line. Once he got going he ran well and began to pursue Gurney, who was leading. He never gave him any real pressure, though, because his gear problems began again and he pulled out on the forty-first lap when part of his drive shaft fell off.

Things were no better at Monza. Jim qualified fourth and ran well for just over a third of the race but then had to retire with a broken piston. Surtees won, closing in on Jim and Hill in the title chase.

The three men arrived at Watkins Glen for the US Grand Prix separated by four points: Graham had thirty-two, Jim thirty and Surtees twenty-eight. Jim's was the fastest car in qualifying and he dominated the race from the start but his fuel injection system went wrong and he had to retire. Lotus called in Spence and gave his car to Jim. He would be unable to score points but he might be able to prevent his rivals from maximising theirs. Initially it seemed to work but Jim had to retire again with eight laps to go because of fuel pump problems.

The European GP at
Brands Hatch in 1964;
Colin Chapman listens
attentively to Jim's
comments about his car.

This left the championship coming down to the last race, the Mexican
Grand Prix on 25 October. Initially the plan was for Jim to run the 25B
but, as practice progressed, he switched to the 33.

Jim had grabbed an important pole and, from the off, the race seemed to be going his way. He made a brilliant start and soon opened up a lead, increasing it steadily with each lap. He was being pursued, seemingly to no avail, by Gurney, Hill, Bandini and Surtees. On the thirty-first lap Hill and Bandini spun off together, letting Surtees through. They managed to keep going but the damage to Hill's car was terminal for his title hopes.

Jim was still leading with seven laps to go and seemed to be in complete command of the championship when he began to realise that he was losing oil. At first it made little difference but by the start of the last lap his car was in too much distress and he stopped; he was officially credited with fifth place. Surtees held on to second and won the title for Ferrari.

A picture of concentration in the cockpit as Jim powers his way to victory at Brands Hatch in 1964.

Victory achieved at Brands Hatch and Jim talks to Colin Chapman as they are besieged by both the press and fans.

Opposite: Jim and Colin with their trophies for winning the European GP at Brands Hatch.

It had been a strange season for Lotus, who had come within minutes of retaining the drivers' championship without really having a reliable car. Their cars were good but the 33 had not quite been ready. However, they knew that once they got past the teething problems they had a winner on their hands. Outside FI, the Lotus Cortina had been a superb success. Jim loved it and his success in the British Saloon Car Championship was good for Lotus's relationship with Ford. It was also good for Jim, because Ford was willing to put a lot of effort into being associated with such a likeable and successful driver.

Indianapolis had been a disaster and Jim, Lotus and Ford were determined not to make sloppy mistakes again. For Colin and Lotus, the FI title was still the main goal but they decided that they would not compete in Monaco next year because it was so close to the Indy 500.

Jim was awarded an O.B.E. the following week. His mother Helen and his sister Betty went with him to Buckingham Palace. On this day of all days, Jim was delayed – he had trouble finding his braces and, naturally,

Like all the greatest
drivers Jim was supreme
in the rain. This shot
shows him pulling away
in the Lotus 33 to victory
at the 1964 Solitude GP
in Stuttgart.

was keen not to have a mishap in the royal presence. The ceremony went well, however, and the Queen commiserated with his bad luck at Mexico.

The 1965 season would be the last year of the 1,500CC FI so it had to be the year in which the Lotus 33 came good, as the 25 had done in 1963.

Instead of being the last race of the season, the South African Grand Prix became the first when it was held on New Year's Day 1965. There were twenty places on the grid, sixteen of them reserved for invitees and four up for grabs in qualifying. One of the new boys that season was Jackie Stewart with the B.R.M. team. Like Jim, Stewart often stayed in John Whitmore's flat in London, so the pair knew each other – indeed, they became close friends. Spence was now a permanent member of Lotus and drove the second car at East London. Jim was in the further-developed 33. The front row consisted of Jim on pole, Surtees and Brabham.

The race started in typical Clark style: quick out of the blocks pulling along team-mate Spence into second from fourth on the grid. Jim

Left: Jim in action in the 1964 Austrian GP. This was the first time it was a world championship event.

Below: Jim with fellow drivers at the Mexican GP, the last of the 1964 season, won by Dan Gurney. Jim came 5th.

Jim having a shot at go-karting at the new Scottish racing circuit at Ingliston in 1964. Although many modern drivers start this way at an early age, this was not an avenue open to Jim who did not begin to compete until after his 17th birthday.

Opposite: Jim sits in the Lotus 33 before the 1965 Race of Champions at Brands Hatch. He was to set the first 100M.P.H. lap for the circuit. Casting a critical eye over the cars is the legendary 'Jenks', Denis Jenkinson, a correspondent for *Motorsport* magazine for many years and who had written about his exploits as Stirling Moss's navigator in the Mille Miglia ten years before in the classic *With Moss in the Mille Miglia.*

gradually pulled out a lead over Spence, who lost his second place after he spun off midway through the race and had to be content with fourth. Jim meanwhile continued on his inexorable way, winning by a thirty-second gap from the Ferrari champion Surtees. This despite a mix-up in which Jim saw the chequered flag come out early, causing him to slow down right at the end of the final lap. Stewart later described it as 'a race won by Jimmy Clark at his most immaculate'.

Within nine days Jim was in Ardmore competing in the New Zealand Grand Prix. It was not a grand prix in the F1 World Championship sense.

These races were always shorter than 200 miles, often just over 100 miles in length, and sometimes run with heats and a final.

Jim was in Australia and New Zealand for two months, competing in the Tasman Series. Lotus ran the Formula 2 set-up 32B with 2.5-litre engines. Jim competed in sixteen races, winning three in New Zealand and two in Australia. Although these were not in the world championship car, it was a very satisfying trip for Jim and the Lotus team.

After this it was back to Europe for more minor races before going off to Indianapolis. Lotus had a new car designed for this year, the Lotus 38, which refined the experiences of the previous two years. It had a new monocoque designed to allow ready access to foot controls from the front of the car. Lola Cars and the British Racing Partnership were now making cars for Indy teams, as were the Americans themselves, and there were very few front-engined cars in the race. There were quite a few Lotus-built cars in the field and more than half of the thirty-three entries used Ford engines. One of the Lotus cars, an older model, was driven by A.J. Foyt,

Opposite: Amidst the hullabaloo of Indianapolis Colin Chapman quietly speaks into Jim's ear as mechanics work on the Lotus 38.

Above: Last minute words from Colin Chapman speaking during practice for the Indy 500.

Above: At full throttle in the Indy 500 on his way to victory. Leading for all but 10 of the 190 laps he set record after record, an overwhelming achievement for a European driver.

Opposite: Jim acknowledges the applause of the crowd at the Indianapolis Motor Speedway.

Overleaf: The team photograph. Posing with the Lotus and Ford mechanics.

who qualified fastest with Jim very close behind him. Gurney was again driving a Lotus but now had his own team, the All American Racers.

The 1965 Indy 500 was a particularly important race for Lotus. The previous year their relationship with Ford had been stretched almost to breaking point when Colin had withdrawn Gurney's car. Moreover, Ford had had to persuade Jim to race: his mother was worried about his safety, his father's health was deteriorating and he was, in fact, considering retiring from racing to devote his time to the farm.

Jim did the same to Indianapolis as he did grand prix racing: he led for 190 of the 200 laps, setting record after record as he blew away the other drivers. He was the first European to win the race in fifty-one years, took away a share of £50,000 (shared with Colin), won at least one overly large trophy and got a glass of milk in Victory Lane. Afterwards, he paid tribute to the team: 'It's not a one-man thing. The amount of work that goes into the race is unbelievable; the number of man hours building the cars and preparing them for the race . . . is fantastic.'

The start of the Belgian GP at Spa. Just two weeks after winning in Indianapolis Jim was confronted with the very wet conditions of a European summer's day. Nevertheless he pulled away from pole to lead for 40 laps, setting the fastest lap time, to win by a convincing margin.

Two weeks later, Jim was back in the FI circus, as was Lotus, who had withdrawn entirely from Monaco when only one entry was guaranteed by the organisers. The third championship grand prix was at Spa, Belgium.

Jim qualified second, sandwiched between the B.R.M.s of Hill and Stewart, but only after tweaking his car's settings. It was raining heavily by the time the race started. Driving into sheets of water, Jim followed Hill through the first bend and then, on the Masta Straight, he leapt into the unknown and pushed his way into the lead. Now with a clear road ahead of him, Jim was able to pull away not by pouring on the gas but by lifting off the accelerator a 'bit less than the others' according to the *Motorsport* race report. Jim slowed down towards the end to conserve his clutch but still finished a lap ahead of everyone except Stewart.

Allan McCall, a Lotus mechanic, once commented on this ability of Jim's to protect his cars. 'Jimmy was so unpunishing with the car,' he said. 'We only had to replace his brake pads after four or five races.'

Another two weeks later was the French Grand Prix at Clermont-Ferrand in the Auvergne. This was the first time a grand prix had been held on the circuit, which was about five miles in length with only one straight, most of the course being a mixture of shallow and sharp bends on the foothills of the Massif Central. Jim had never driven at Clermont before and could manage only fifth fastest on the first day of practice. The next day, like everyone else, he significantly increased his speed, taking pole. Hill was back on the fifth row, having spun into the rocks on Friday.

Despite driving a car with an old engine that required careful handling, Jim led from start to finish. Stewart was again second but couldn't mount a serious challenge for the lead.

Side by side in the paddock at Spa, the Lotus 33s of Jim and Mike Spence – though their race numbers were to be 6 and 8.

Below: The goggles go on as Jim prepares for the 1965 French GP at Clermont-Ferrand.

Opposite: Jim leading the French GP with a seemingly empty track behind him. In another immaculate display of his driving skills he led from pole for all 40 laps, setting the fastest lap time and winning with a margin of nearly half-a-minute from Jackie Stewart.

The British Grand Prix at Silverstone was sponsored by the *Daily Express*, which labelled it 'the return of power' and used an anachronistic poster showing a front-engined car. Six years of rear-engined racing cars and it looked as if the newspapers hadn't noticed.

On the second day of practice, Jim received the new Cosworth Climax 32-valve engine. He took pole, exchanging fastest times with Hill, who was second. Richie Ginther qualified third in a Honda and challenged Jim for the lead on the first lap – he actually beat Jim to the first bend but Jim passed him on the Hangar Straight. He was then able gradually to pull out a big lead; not even Hill or Surtees could keep up.

The race was turned on its end after the fiftieth lap, when Jim's car began to lose power and oil. To conserve his engine he had to back off the throttle and even switched off the engine in right-handers to protect his falling oil pressure, and his thirty-second lead began to look precarious. By the end, Hill was in his mirrors and Jim won by a little over three seconds.

Eight days later it was back to Zandvoort for the Dutch Grand Prix, the sixth of the season and Jim's fifth. Jim qualified behind Hill, with Ginther in the Honda on third. For the second time in succession, Ginther seized the lead at the start, holding it until the third lap, when Hill passed him. Jim took the lead a few laps later. His winning margin was eight seconds over Stewart. It was his fifth successive win.

Lotus again invited Mitter onto the team for the German Grand Prix at the Nürburgring. Stewart initially led the practice times but Jim, in the afternoon, set the pole time of 8 minutes 22.7 seconds. It was so dominant that he had no need to try to improve it in final practice on the Saturday. Stewart has since said that, 'Jimmy always seemed to be one step ahead of me.' Behind Jim were Stewart, Hill and Surtees, with Spence's Lotus in the middle of the second row on the grid.

David Jenkins' reports on recent grands prix had been bemoaning the intrusion of television cameras into the pits and even into the practice schedules. Cars had gone out onto the track purely for the benefit of the cameras. The situation at this race was very different. Jenkins' report in *Motorsport* describes seven cameras around the circuit. The Nürburgring was fourteen miles long, so once the cars left the stadium section they were out of touch from the pits until they reappeared eight minutes later. Cameras not only allowed the teams to time their drivers and measure their lead or deficit

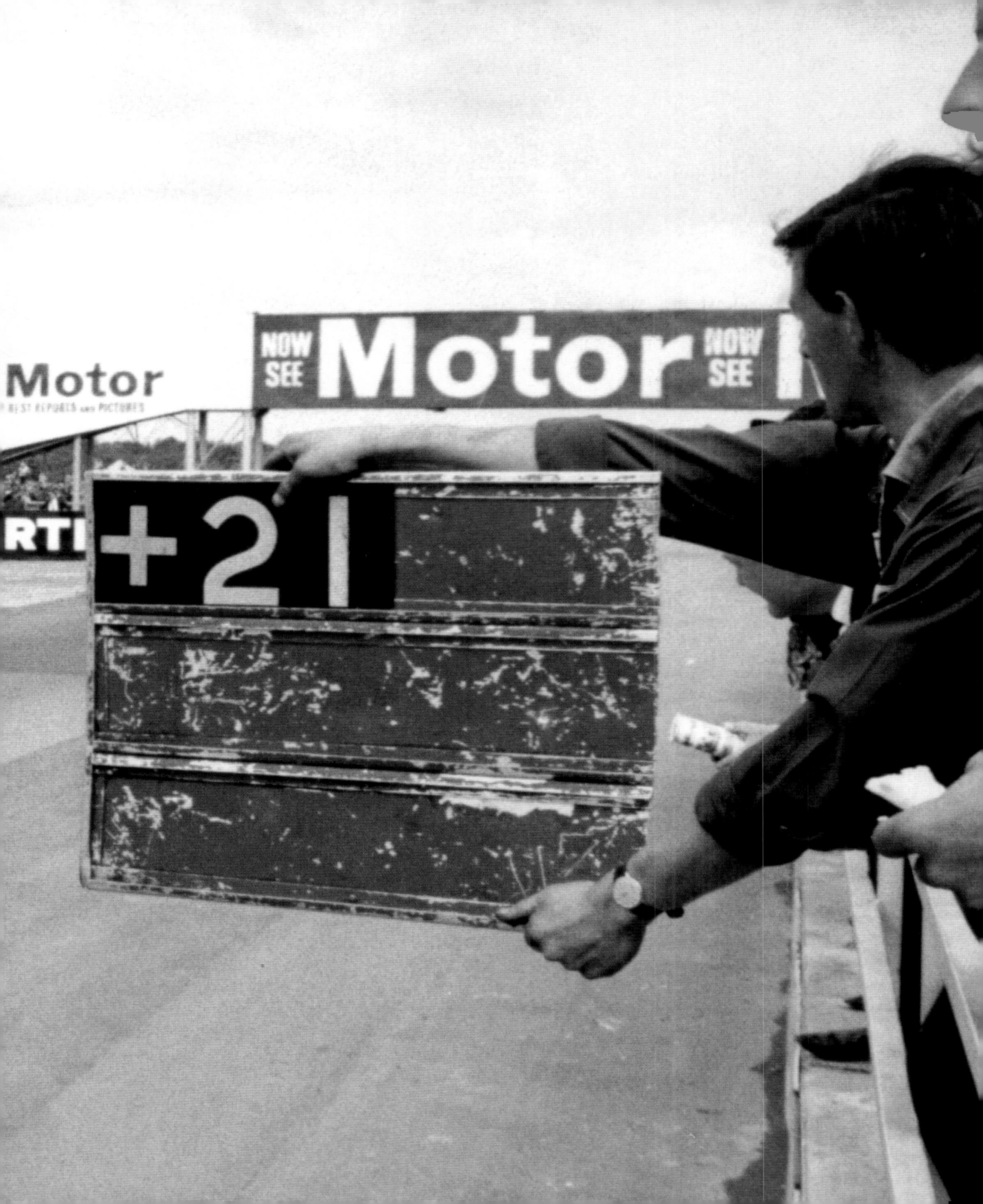
Motor
NOW SEE
Motor
NOW SEE
+21

Six pages of action at the 1965 British Grand Prix at Silverstone

Previous four pages: The start of the 1965 British GP with Jim on the left in the new Cosworth Climax-engined Lotus and Richie Ginther in the Honda on the right.

In the middle of a devastating sequence of 5 grand prix wins in a row Jim led all 80 laps of the race from pole. After building up a commanding lead (the middle spread shows a Lotus mechanic signalling a 21 second lead) on the 50th lap, the new engine began to lose power and as Graham Hill closed the gap the Lotus limped over the line just over 3 seconds ahead.

Right: Jim poses for the cameras. Another British GP, another win for a popular driver.

Jim in the pits during the 1965 Dutch GP weekend conferring with Colin Chapman.

against rivals but also enabled them to amend their strategies throughout the race. Of course, the cars had no radios back then and drivers still had to read their pitboards each lap.

Whether all this helped Jim is unclear because the race was typical of him. He was quick off the grid and into the lead by the first corner, able to keep the pressure on to the end, winning by fifteen seconds. It was his sixth win of the season and Jim was virtually assured of regaining the title.

The Italian Grand Prix at Monza in September was the most competitive race so far. Lotus fielded three cars, having given one to a young Italian driver nicknamed 'Geki'. Qualifying was strongly contested, with financial prizes on offer for the fastest qualifiers on each day. Jim took pole with Surtees' Ferrari and Stewart's B.R.M. making up the front row. Hill's B.R.M. was on the second row with Bandini's Ferrari.

Jim was unable to seize the lead decisively and was part of a group of seven cars constantly swapping places at the front. The weaker Brabhams and Ferraris were unable to make any real impression and Surtees

dropped back with clutch problems, though he got back on terms after a few laps, before having to withdraw when his clutch failed completely.

Clark, Stewart and Hill fought over the lead. All was well with Jim's car until lap sixty-three, when electrical problems caused his fuel pump to fail and he was out. Stewart went on to take the first of his many FI victories.

The grand prix at Watkins Glen in the US was another disappointing race for Jim. He qualified second behind Hill, despite having done the fastest time in qualifying in Spence's Lotus. He also managed to show some fallibility by going off the course in full of view of the mechanics. In the race itself, he started well and led from the second lap until he retired on the twelfth, leaving the race to Hill for the third year in succession.

Jim kneeling to talk to Lotus team mate Mike Spence during qualification for the 1965 Dutch GP.

Above: The start of the 1965 Dutch GP. Richie Ginther's Honda holds a short-lived lead. Jim went on to lead for 75 of the 80 laps and set the fastest lap time for his 5th win of the season.

Right: A Lotus mechanic holds up a board to show that Jim has a 27-second lead on lap 3 of the 1965 German GP.

The Duns Town Council marked Jim's achievements by making him burgess of Duns, the first since Duns got its charter in 1489. The celebrations included a showing of Jim's Indy 500 win, an open-topped bus tour, with police escort, and a menu that featured omelette surprise.

The last race of the year, the Mexican Grand Prix was another poor one for Jim. He took pole with his spare car after his original car's engine blew in practice. Gurney was alongside him on the grid, with Ginther's Honda on the second row. Ginther made the best start, pulling out into the lead and taking Honda's first victory. Jim made it only as far as the ninth lap, pulling off the circuit near the hairpin at the farthest point from the pits.

Despite the disappointing end to the season, Jim had totally dominated the championship and secured his second title with fifty-four points to Hill's forty. Lotus again took the constructors' title. Add in the Indy 500 win and it had been a particularly successful season.

Jim leading the field out of the South Curve on the Nürburgring. He led from pole to flag on his way to his 6th win, setting fastest lap once again as he clinched his second world championship and Lotus the Constructors' Championship.

Jim's Lotus-Climax closely pursues Jackie Stewart's B.R.M. at the 1965 Italian Grand Prix at Monza. At first it looked like another procession for Jim starting from pole position and setting the fastest lap but he retired after 63 of the 76 laps with a faulty fuel pump. This was Jackie's first Grand Prix victory.

Chapter 5
Developing the 49

AT THE END OF 1965 Jim was at the height of his career but by no means at the pinnacle of his talents. Colin Chapman's creative spark still had plenty of energy left, too. Coupled with this was the motivating factor that adversity is a great spur to genius. Technology and competition were increasing in Formula 1 and what had been good enough for the past would not do for the future. For 1966 the regulations governing F1 were undergoing a major revision: the 1.5-litre limit was going. Now, teams were allowed to enter up to 3-litre unsupercharged engines or 1.5-litre engines with superchargers.

Jim was a world-class racing driver but probably no more than an average amateur mechanic. According to Bob Dance's memory, Jim didn't visit the factory much. When he did visit, it was to discuss racing business or be fitted to the cars as they were being built. His contribution lay very much in driving the cars and feeding back information to Colin and his team. Jim once described the relationship thus: 'I tell [Colin] what is wanted with the car and he works out how to do it.'

In Bob's eye, this lack of mechanical understanding was Jim's greatest weakness but also his strength: if the car stood any chance of winning, Jim could make it win. If he had to hold the gear stick awkwardly, he could do so and still be quicker than anyone. He was a genius; not just very good – a genius. That was all well and good but it must have been a frustrating experience for his team-mates.

Jim celebrates his team mate Trevor Taylor's win in the 1962 Natal GP.

A new car was needed for 1966. It would still be a monocoque, because that was where the future lay for FI, but it would need to take a bigger and more powerful engine.

Coventry Climax had withdrawn from FI and Chapman had to find a new engine manufacturer to work with. Luckily he had some obvious avenues to explore. The relationship that he had formed with Ford over the Indy 500 projects now moved into the area of grand prix racing. Ford didn't develop an engine directly for Lotus, but was happy to provide the finance for one. Colin turned to Cosworth Engineering, a firm he knew well. Mike Costin – co-founder of Cosworth – was a former employee of Lotus. Colin commissioned Cosworth to produce a v8 for FI but it would not be ready in time for the start of the season.

Therefore, Colin decided that Lotus would purchase the new B.R.M. engine, which B.R.M. would be using in its own cars. However, these were not readily adaptable to fit the Lotus 33, so Lotus bought some old Coventry Climax v8 engines with large bores that would crankshaft from smaller bore engines. These 2-litre engines produced 240B.H.P., which was less than the 400B.H.P. that Lotus wanted but at least it gave them an engine that they could compete with.

Another problem was a lack of FI races in Britain. In previous years there had been a full calendar of minor races throughout England and elsewhere, allowing the teams to fine-tune their cars.

Jim missed the first grand prix, which was held in South Africa on 1 January, because he was racing in New Zealand and Australia. But Lotus had two other entrants in this non-championship race and they achieved some encouraging results. Mike Spence won in the 2-litre Lotus 33 and Peter Arundell – returning to competitive driving after missing most of 1965 while he recovered from an injury sustained in a Formula 2 race at Reims in 1964 – came third in the previous season's car.

Jim was a world-class racing driver but probably no more than an average amateur mechanic. His contribution lay in driving the cars and feeding back information to Colin Chapman. Jim once described the relationship thus: 'I tell Colin what is wanted with the car and he works out how to do it.' If a car stood any chance of winning, Jim could make it win. He was a genius; not just very good – a genius.

Jim managed to finish only one of his races in New Zealand, where he came second. The Tasman Series in Australia was more successful: he won the first race at Sydney and came in the top three in the next two races. It was a happy time, though, relaxing and playing sports with Graham Hill, Jackie Stewart and Dick Attwood.

Back in Europe, the championship season got going in May with the Monaco Grand Prix. Stewart was quickest on the first day of qualifying,

Previous pages: Jim in the pits with rival drivers Jackie Stewart and Graham Hill, both from B.R.M., at the Monaco GP of 1966.

Above: Jim skirts the harbour in Monaco in the Lotus 33.

but on the following two days Jim got quicker and quicker, seizing pole position with a time of 1 minute 29.9 seconds, a little over one and a half seconds quicker than Stewart.

At the start of the race, Jim found himself stuck in first gear and dropped to the back of the field. As was his habit, he made good progress and by lap twenty had began to make his presence felt on the leaders. He eventually got into third place after overtaking Hill on lap sixty-one but then a mechanical failure caused him to spin off and out of the race.

Jim's next race was the Indy 500 and, while he was not to win it, he demonstrated his amazing driving skills when in adversity: he spun twice, on both occasions managing to regain control. According to Bob, 'If you spun at Indy, the wall seemed to claim you. Jim was probably the only man to spin there and not hit anything.'

For much of the earlier part of the race, after Mario Andretti dropped out, Jim was leading and at one point he, Hill and Stewart occupied the first three places. Hill eventually won with Jim behind him in second place, partly because of faulty pit signals that told Jim he was leading when he wasn't. He and Hill remained good friends, though, and put it behind them with a party to celebrate Hill's win at Graham and his wife's house in London, where they exchanged racing stories with Stirling Moss.

Jim's experiences in Monaco may have been mixed but there were no redeeming features at all at Spa. He was driving the Lotus 33 with the 2-litre engine and in first practice set a time that put him on the fourth row of the grid. Spence had now left Lotus and Arundell was Jim's full-time team-mate. Arundell was attempting to qualify in the new Lotus with the

Guy Ligier in a Cooper-Maserati leads the middle of the pack round the Racasse at Monaco in 1966. Jim is only just in shot, the fourth in this group. He retired with suspension problems despite having started from pole position. The race was filmed for footage for the cult movie *Grand Prix* which won several Oscars.

B.R.M. engine, but it broke down and couldn't be repaired. Lotus had no other cars available, so he was out of the grand prix after just a few qualifying laps. At one point, Jim's chances looked no better: he was unable to practice on the Saturday and couldn't beat his Friday time.

Qualifying may have seemed bad but the race was a disaster. It was a wet day and there was standing water on the circuit – potentially treacherous on a circuit such as Spa. John Surtees took an early lead and Jim overcooked his engine attempting to get back into the fray and went out on the first lap. A number of people spun in the wet conditions, including Stewart, who was trapped in his car with petrol spilling into the cockpit. Half the field failed to survive the first lap.

Opposite: Jim sits hunched in the pits at the Indianapolis 500 race in 1966. He finished 2nd.

Above: Jim and Sally Stokes, his then girlfriend, receiving a Ford Galaxy as part of the prize for his Indy 500 victory in 1965.

Jim, as the winner in 1965, acknowledges the applause of the crowd at the 1966 Indy '500'.

Above: Despite at this point being ahead of the eventual winner, Jim crashed out on the first lap of the 1966 Belgian GP.

Opposite: Graham Hill leads Jim uphill in the 1966 British GP. Jim finished 4th, just behind Hill who came 3rd.

After this came the French Grand Prix, on 3 July at Reims. Jim's and Lotus's luck just seemed to get worse. Arundell didn't practice on Wednesday and on Thursday didn't even manage to complete one lap before burning his clutch. Eventually, in final practice, he did set a qualifying time so that the Lotus 43 with a B.R.M. engine would get a race start under its belt, but then his gearbox failed.

At least he made it to the start. Jim set two moderate times and then was hit in the face by a bird, damaging his left eye and putting him out of the race completely.

The next grand prix, two weeks later, was the British one, held at Brands Hatch. Both Jim and Arundell were driving 33s, Jim's with a

The 1966 Dutch GP at
Zandvoort saw Jim finish
in third after water pump
problems in the Lotus 33.
In this photograph early
in the race he is lying 2nd
behind eventual winner
Jack Brabham.

Lotus mechanics top up the water on Jim's overheating car at Zandvoort in 1966.

Above: The cockpit of
Jim's Lotus 43 at Monza
in 1966. The gear lever
can just be seen on the
right of the photograph.

Opposite: Jim practising
in Giacomo Russo's
(known by the
pseudonym 'Geki') Lotus
43 B.R.M.. at Monza. This
was the first outing for
the 43 with the B.R.M.
H16 engine. Jim retired
with gearbox problems
ten laps from the end.

Coventry Climax engine and Arundell's modified
to take the B.R.M. engine, which he was unable to
practice with until Friday.

Jim was late arriving for the first practice
session because of having to be cleared to drive
following his head injuries from France. His
vision was pronounced fit for racing and he did
eventually get going. Stewart was also returning
after his crash at Spa – despite his injuries he
missed only one grand prix.

Qualifying was dominated by the cars of Jack
Brabham's eponymous team, which qualified on
pole and second. Jim was fifth, one tenth of a
second behind Hill. At times during the race, Jim
was blazing around the circuit incredibly quickly:
he recorded the second-fastest lap of the race.
But with his underpowered car he was more
occupied with duelling for position with Hill.

Brabham and Denny Hulme, the second
Brabham driver, eventually pulled away from the
others and finished a lap ahead of Clark and Hill.
Hill's car had taken structural damage on the first
lap and later developed low oil pressure and Jim had begun to lose braking
power and, just after mid distance, had had to make a hasty pitstop to have
his brake fluid topped up, so they'd done well to finish third and fourth.

A week later, at the Dutch Grand Prix, Jim again had to take a back seat
in qualifying: Jack Brabham and Hulme occupied the first two positions
on the grid and Jim was third, taking the final position on the first row.
Brabham took the lead from the start and Jim managed to get past Hulme
into second. He temporarily lost position but then regained it when the
second Brabham began to develop ignition problems, which eventually
dropped it out of the race.

Jack Brabham hit trouble on lap twenty-seven and Jim went past. He
began to stretch out a bit of lead for the first time this season. His glory
was short-lived, however, because his engine began to vibrate badly and
he had to ease off the power. Then the water pump broke and Jim had to
dive into the pits, for the second race in succession, for a quick top-up,
this time for water. He rejoined to finish third behind Hill's B.R.M.

The German Grand Prix was held at the Nürburgring on 7 August and,
due to a shortage of entries, the event was combined with the meeting's
F2 race to provide more of a spectacle for the fans. This time, Jim qualified
on pole – an incredible feat in an underpowered car with a cobbled-
together engine. The machinery wasn't up to the job, however: Jim lost

For the Italian Grand Prix in September, Lotus finally had its B.R.M. engine and the Lotus 43 could make its race début in Jim's hands. It ran very smoothly in qualifying but had minor problems with its gearbox. In the race, however, Jim never got into a position to challenge even for the minor points.

Previous pages: The start
of the 1966 US GP. Jim
recorded his only GP
success here in 1966 and
the only success for the
powerful but unreliable
B.R.M. H16 engine.

Above: Jim sits in the
Lotus 43 B.R.M. in the
paddock at the 1966
Mexico GP.

the lead at the start of the race and dropped back through the field before
crashing on lap twelve out of fifteen.

For the Italian Grand Prix in September, Lotus finally had its B.R.M.
engine and the Lotus 43 could make its race début in Jim's hands. It ran
very smoothly in qualifying, although it did have minor problems with
its gearbox. Jim qualified third, behind the two Ferraris driven by Mike
Parkes and Ludovico Scarfiotti. However, when the race started he was
left on line, perhaps having been held there for too long. He moved back
through the field and begin to challenge his rivals but on lap thirteen he
was forced into the pits for a tyre change, which dropped him to last place.

Although he was still able to run very quickly after this, Jim never got
back into a position to challenge even for the minor points. He did manage
to catch the leader, Scarfiotti, and unlap himself but it was all futile. By lap
fifty-nine, nine from the end, he had to retire with a broken gearbox.
Meanwhile, Jack Brabham clinched the championship.

Colin entered three Lotuses for the US Grand Prix at Watkins Glen, the third car to be driven by Pedro Rodriguez. On the first day of practice Jim was quick, managing 1 minute 10 seconds, just over a second slower than Lorenzo Bandini in the Ferrari, but was only eighth-fastest at this point. Just at the end of final practice on the Saturday, he got his quickest time down to 1 minute 8.53 seconds for second place on the grid beside Jack Brabham. However, this came at the expense of breaking his engine, which – luckily – Lotus was able to replace with the spare B.R.M. engine, which they did not need for the race.

The race itself ended in victory for Jim, but it was not taken in his usual style. Bandini's Ferrari leaped from third on the grid into the lead, followed by Jim's Lotus. But after only a few laps Jim had dropped to fourth behind Brabham and Surtees. The B.R.M. H16 engine was running smoothly but he didn't trouble the leaders again until lap fifty-six. Meanwhile, Bandini's engine failed on lap thirty-five and Brabham took over the lead – until he, too, had an engine failure, which allowed Jim into the lead and the win.

The final race of the season was held on 23 October at Mexico City. Because only three weeks had elapsed since the US Grand Prix, none of the Lotus cars had been back to the factory: they were sent straight from Watkins Glen to Mexico. The cars were harder to set up for this race because of the city's altitude: the fuel suffered from greater loss and poorer efficiency due to vaporisation.

Jim drove the car that had gone so smoothly for him in America and ended up second on the grid. However, at the end of the first practice session the bolts in the crankshaft broke, so he needed a new engine.

The race itself was one of frustration and he never really got going. He had gear problems that quickly dropped him down the order and by lap ten he had retired from the unequal contest. The race was won by Surtees in the Cooper-Maserati.

It had been a miserable season for Jim and for Lotus, a total contrast to the previous year, when the 33 had been supremely reliable. Coventry Climax's withdrawal from F1 had left Lotus unable to undertake any engine development and the team had ended up running two temporary engines that were never going to be taken forward. The outcome was therefore probably not surprising but Jim was no longer a rookie driver uncertain of his ability. When the cars ran well, he had shown enough of his real ability to ease his wounded pride. But this was the first season since 1961 that he had not been in contention for the championship.

It is often said that Colin's cars were prone to falling apart, his philosophy being that the car should be designed to reach the end of the race and no more. Even then it was apparent that when Jim failed to finish a race, it was usually because of the car, not driver error. Jim once

Above: Jim's Cortina MKI in the 1966 RAC rally. Jim did not finish. Stirling Moss's sister, Pat Moss-Carlsson came 9th out of 144 starters.

Opposite: A publicity shot of Jim serving petrol at the Northern Garage that he bought at Tweedmouth, just outside Berwick-upon-Tweed.

told Colin, 'Build a car that is going to hold together and I'll drive it. But if I think it is going to fall apart, I am going to be two seconds a lap slower.'

The 1966 season was also notable for another reason: although money was not the motivating force behind Jim's racing, he was really starting to earn well. He had developed new income streams outside racing; he'd even been photographed by David Bailey with the model Jean Shrimpton.

All this meant that Jim was moving into the highest tax brackets and his financial advisors suggested reorganising his tax liabilities. He eventually, reluctantly, became a tax exile. At first he moved to Paris to stay in Jabby Crombac's flat. This was a very half-hearted move, however, showing that he really had no wish to distance himself from his homeland. John Whitmore's flat in London, which Jim and Stewart stayed in, had even become known as the 'Scottish embassy' by Jim and fellow-Scot Stewart. The move to Paris was hardly sufficient to convince the British Inland

Revenue that Jim had moved out of its clutches. Eventually, at the end of 1966, he bought a house in Bermuda.

Following the end of the F1 season, Jim turned his hand back to rallying. Some people may have seen it as a bit of a stunt but for Jim it was just another form of motorsport and one in which he already had a successful record. A Lotus Cortina won the rally, but this time it was not Jim's – he overturned his three-quarters of the way through, but not before demonstrating that he had lost none of his skill.

For 1967, the rules for deciding the F1 World Championship changed. Previously, drivers had been able to discard their worst results when allocating championship points. Now, the championship would be divided into two sections: the South African Grand Prix was reinstated in January and became the first event of the first segment, which would finish with the

'Build a car that is going to hold together and I'll drive it. But if I think it is going to fall apart, I am going to be two seconds a lap slower.' — Jim Clark to Colin Chapman

Jim coming down the hill past the Hotel Mirabeau at Monaco in 1967. Having set the fastest lap he retired with suspension problems before the half-way mark.

British Grand Prix and consist of six races. The last five races would make up the second segment, from the German to the Mexican Grand Prix. Drivers could discard their points from one race in each section. This meant that, to be successful, teams and drivers would have to perform consistently throughout the season.

More immediately important for Jim and the team, Lotus once again made a huge technical step forward that would enhance F1 for years to come. The Ford-financed Cosworth D.F.V. V8 engine made its début during the season and, in 1967, Lotus was the only team to have it. The engine would become more widely available from the next season and, indeed, would go on to dominate F1 for fifteen years.

The first race was on 2 January at Kyalami, just outside Johannesburg. Arundell had been replaced at Lotus by Hill, who had previously been a Lotus driver before joining B.R.M. in 1959. For now, the team still had to run the B.R.M. H16-engined Lotus 43. The plan was for the Cosworth engines to be used from the start of the European season at Monte Carlo.

This was the first time that Lotus had produced an F1 chassis design with an accompanying engine. The car was the 49 and would go on to be one of Lotus's most successful racing cars, but it was too much to hope that it would be free of teething problems. It had, however, played its role in enabling Lotus to entice Hill away from B.R.M.

The Lotus garage at
Indianapolis.

Kyalami is at an altitude of 5,000 feet, giving rise to similar set-up
problems to those at Mexico City. Not ideal if you're running a new car
and getting to know it.

In first practice, Jim was about four seconds off the pace because he was
breaking in a new chassis. The next day he got quicker, taking one point
seven seconds off his previous quickest time. The improvements continued
during final practice as Jim grew more accustomed to his new equipment,
found its strengths and gained confidence with it. Even so, he managed
only 1 minute 29 seconds, good enough only for the second row.

Hill had a terrible time in practice and lasted only to the seventh lap of
the race, when he had an accident. Jim did better but was unable to keep
up with the leaders and by lap nineteen his Lotus was overheating, forcing
him out three laps later.

After this first there was a gap before the European tour began in May in Monaco. Before that Lotus, as usual, took part in the Tasman races in Australia and New Zealand.

Lotus's new car still was not ready for Monaco: Jim was in the previous year's 33 with a Coventry Climax and Hill had one with the B.R.M. engine. However, due to transport problems, they missed the first practice session. With two practice sessions remaining, on the Friday and Saturday, Jim was able only to get onto the third row of the grid, a little more than a second down on Brabham's pole time. On a narrow track such as Monaco, where overtaking is extremely difficult, this virtually forced him to wait for pitstops and retirements to move through the field.

Brabham overcooked his start and his engine broke a connecting rod, spilling oil onto the circuit. Then he spun, causing the pack to take evasive action. When they came around on the second lap Jim was preparing to avoid an accident on the oil patch. Nothing actually happened, except that

When Graham Hill returned to Lotus in 1967 he did not just form a successful driving partnership with Jim but along with Colin Chapman formed a trio with a formidable knowledge of and skill in the art of Formula 1 motor racing.

Stewart took the lead from Bandini's Ferrari and Jim shot onto the escape road; he had to reverse out of it into fourteenth and last place. Thanks to retirements and his own pace, Jim began to move back through the field, setting fastest laps as he overtook Courage's B.R.M. and Rodriguez's Cooper Maserati within a few laps. Eventually he made his way up to fourth place but, as he entered the Tabac on the forty-third lap, a rear shock absorber broke and spun his car into the wall.

On a positive note for Lotus, Hill came second, demonstrating that the car could be reliable even on F1's toughest circuit.

Next up was the Indy 500, but Jim had probably his least competitive attempt at the race. He had been a mould breaker there in 1965 but this year he qualified poorly and retired early with a broken piston.

By the time of the Dutch Grand Prix at Zandvoort, in early June, Lotus finally had two 49s ready with the Cosworth D.F.V. There were three practice sessions on the Friday, by the end of which Jim was still rather off the pace. His car was brand new: he'd seen it for the first time only that morning and he was unhappy with the set-up. On the Saturday, with very

'It was quite alarming. I was going down the straight swinging the steering from one side to the other, trying to keep the car on the road.' — Jim Clark

little found to be wrong, he went out again but a ball-race failed in the right-rear hub. He got back out later but was unable to improve on his quickest time and ended up eighth, on the third row of the grid.

Hill got away well from pole. There was still an official on the grid when the flag was dropped and Jim took advantage of the confusion this caused to move into sixth position. His car had been fitted with different tyres and wheel springs after Hill's successful practice but this meant that Jim had very little experience of the car he was driving. He later described it as 'quite alarming. I was going down the straight swinging the steering from one side to the other, trying to keep the car on the road.'

Hill quickly opened out a lead but was unable to break clear from the field and on lap twelve he was forced out of the race with a broken camshaft. Jim was running fourth and soon passed Jochen Rindt and Brabham to move into the lead.

Within a few laps he was opening out a healthy lead – it was up to eleven seconds and increasing by about the halfway stage. Lotus seemed to have found the winning formula, if only they could keep the engine running and Jim behind the wheel. Reliability was clearly still a worry,

Opposite: At Zandvoort in 1967, a view of the new Ford Cosworth DFV engine in the Lotus 49 with which Jim set fastest lap and won the race nearly 25 seconds ahead of Jack Brabham. If he had lived Jim would undoubtedly have used the power and reliability of the car to take him to his third world championship.

Previous pages: The start of the 1967 French GP at Le Mans. Jim's Lotus 49 is on the second row nearest the camera.

Above: Jim waving to the crowds at Silverstone after winning his final British GP in 1967.

however. But Jim kept going and took the chequered flag almost twenty-five seconds ahead of Brabham.

Jim's sister Betty Peddie was at the race. Afterwards, she and Jim spent time with his ex-girlfriend Sally Stokes and her husband Eddy Swartz. Sally had probably been the love of Jim's life and was very popular with his family – she is still in touch with them now. But Jim's attitude was that marriage and racing didn't mix and he was determined not to marry until after he retired from driving. Sally was his girlfriend for two or three years but eventually she could wait no longer and she married Eddy in 1967. Their other problem had been Sally's habitual lack of punctuality. As someone who was in demand by sponsors and motoring clubs, Jim needed to be on time for social events. But it was his inability to commit to the relationship long-term that broke them apart. Sally and Jim remained friends, however, so there was no uneasiness at Zandvoort and, indeed, they spent much of the evening after the race dancing and chatting.

Ian Scott Watson remembers being with Jim and his new girlfriend in London one day. As they turned into a car park, Jim spotted one of his cars, which he had allowed to Sally to keep, so rather than embarrass her he changed their plans and he and Ian went somewhere else.

The next championship race was in Belgium. Jim's performance at Zandvoort had seemed an indicator of things to come. Now the fast straights and bends of Spa would provide a good test of the new car's speed and road-handling qualities.

Both cars were exceptionally fast in qualifying, although Hill's suffered from engine problems on the Saturday. Jim, on the other hand, was in rampant form and only Dan Gurney's Eagle-Weslake was in any way competitive – and that was still almost three seconds a lap slower than Jim's Lotus. Jim set his quickest lap right at the end of practice on Saturday, having been balked by the slower Ferraris of Amon and Scarfiotti, and with a sticking throttle, and yet he still set a lap of 3 minutes 28.1 seconds. That's an average of just over 150M.P.H. on a very dangerous circuit with a first-gear hairpin.

1967 was the only year that Clark competed in the Canadian GP. After achieving pole position and setting the fastest lap he retired on lap 69 with ignition problems.

The Lotus 49 airborne at
the Flugplatz on the
Nürburgring in 1967.
From pole position he
retired on lap 4, once
again with suspension
problems.

Jim relaxing in the pit lane at Monza in 1967. This race is remembered as one of the most exciting of all time. Jim started on pole, set the fastest lap, had to pit to replace a tyre, drove hard from a lap adrift to retake the lead and held it to the 68th and last lap when he ran out of fuel, to be overtaken by Brabham and Surtees who fought their own duel to cross the line almost neck and neck.

Jim, carrying a flat tyre, is passed by Jack Brabham early in the 1967 Italian Grand Prix.

Hill and Gurney started the race badly. Hill didn't even make it to the grid: he drained his battery and had to roll into the pits. This left Jim at the front ready to pick up where he had left off at Zandvoort. Stewart's B.R.M. was unable to cut into his lead and by lap ten Jim's lead was twenty-one seconds. Deliverance was at hand for Jim's pursuers, however: on lap twelve he came into the pits with a defective spark plug. It could be fixed but he had to come in again later for another one. Then he suffered gearbox problems and was able to finish only sixth, a lap behind Gurney, who had got ahead of Stewart when he also had gear-selection problems.

The next race was the French Grand Prix in early July. This year it was held at the Bugatti Au Mans circuit, featuring the start-finish straight that is used in the 24-hour race with a shorter, twisty section of track totalling almost three miles in length. This layout was not so popular with the spectators, who had naturally come to expect high-speed running at Le Mans, which this modified version of the track would not allow. On the start-finish straight the speeds were half what they might have been

had the cars been coming down from the 'White House' on the 24-hour track: only about 80M.P.H.

The entry for the race was much reduced, too. Ferrari had only one car and Honda didn't bother at all. However, both Lotuses were there, although the cars did not actually arrive in time for the first of two days of practice and qualifying. On the Saturday, neither Lotus ran well, although Hill's performed better than Jim's. Hill took pole position and Jim had to be content with fourth on the grid.

The race itself initially went well for Lotus. Hill led for a while, then Jim took the lead on lap five. He retained it until lap eleven, when Hill went ahead again. Three laps later Hill retired with gear problems; the same problem forced Jim out after twenty-four laps. It must have been particularly galling for Lotus because they had had minimal practice and yet had been totally dominating the race. Brabham won from his second driver, Hulme, who was just over a minute behind him.

The two Lotus cars run side by side at Monza, Jim on the left and Graham Hill on the right. Hill retired with engine problems 10 laps from the finish.

Before the British Grand Prix on 15 July, Lotus did a lot of work to improve its ZF gearboxes. Jim set the fastest lap on the Thursday despite having an engine that was constantly misfiring due to an overly rich fuel mixture. On Friday, with the car functioning properly, he went faster and faster, knocking 1.2 seconds off the previous day's fastest time. Hill also came on stronger and finished second on the grid before a mechanical failure caused him to crash in the pitlane, virtually writing off the car. Luckily, because this happened in Britain, the Lotus mechanics were able to complete the Lotus 49/3 in the factory in Norwich, with the useable bits from the car at Silverstone, so he had a car for the race.

The race itself was a demonstration of Lotus power. Jim led for the first twenty-six laps with Hill right behind him, then Hill took over for the next twenty-nine laps until his suspension collapsed just as it had done in practice. Jim won by thirteen seconds over Hulme's Brabham.

'I think the most important thing in motor racing is concentration. If I want to go faster, I don't drive any faster; I just concentrate harder.' — Jim Clark

The German Grand Prix in August was again a combined F1 and F2 race and was another frustrating race for Jim and Lotus. Jim was quickest in practice by ten seconds, not at all bad in a car with an overly effective braking system that was spoiling its handling. In the race itself, he led from the off but only until lap five, when his suspension collapsed. Hill suffered the same fate four laps later.

Next, the teams headed off to Toronto for the Canadian Grand Prix. Again the Lotuses were the fastest cars in practice. Jim and Hill qualified on the front row with Hulme.

Conditions during practice had been dry but a constant drizzle fell on race day. Jim led for the first three laps but was passed by Hulme on lap four. He ran at the front of the pack until problems forced him out of the race after sixty-nine laps.

The next race, at Monza on 10 September, was one of Jim's greatest-ever drives. Lotus ran three cars, the third one being given to the Italian driver Giancarlo Baghetti. Initially Jim struggled in practice because his gear ratios were unsuitable. Then he went out in Baghetti's car but the Italian's driving position was not to his liking and he was unable to set any fast times. However, in typical Jim Clark style, once his own car was ready he went out and set the fastest time of first practice in 1 minute 28.5 seconds. The second day was spoiled by torrential rain and hail and no one was able to match Jim's time from the previous day. Jim was on pole ahead of Brabham and Bruce McLaren.

There was confusion at the start of the race while the cars stood on the dummy grid. They should have been signalled forward onto the grid proper, but no signal was forthcoming. Brabham and McLaren revved their engines in anticipation of a full-blooded racing start. Jim got caught out and Gurney came through from the second row, passing McLaren. This left Brabham in the lead, but he lost it to Gurney before the end of the lap. They were hotly pursued by Hill and Clark. By the end of the second lap Jim had got past Hill and Brabham into second place and on the following lap he took the lead. Gurney dropped out two laps later, leaving Jim leading from his team-mate. However, at this point Jim's Lotus began to lose its handling and the chasing cars started to close in on him. He lost the lead momentarily to Hulme and by lap twelve he knew that his right-rear tyre was gradually going flat.

Jim pitted for a new tyre and rejoined the race in fifteenth place, more than a lap down on the leaders. Brabham and Hulme were disputing the lead and lapping in 1 minute 30 seconds but Jim was already beginning to close up on them, having made it up to eleventh over the course of a few laps. Soon he was right behind the leaders, then he unlapped himself and started pulling away from them.

Just before the halfway stage, Hill managed to take the lead from Hulme, who soon dropped out, and was opening up a big gap ahead of Brabham. At the halfway point, the three Lotus cars were running together with Jim leading them around on the track, although he was actually almost a lap behind Hill.

Baghetti eventually dropped back, leaving Jim and Graham out on their own, with Hill being pulled around in the slipstream of his team-mate's car. Jim was eating into the gap between himself and all the cars ahead of him and it seemed that all Hill had to do to win was keep running, such was the pace that Jim was setting.

However, Hill's engine gave out when Jim was closing in on Brabham. Jim soon took the lead and began to open out a commanding gap. Surtees took over second place on the sixty-fifth lap, where he stayed until they entered the final lap, when Jim's Lotus began to suffer engine problems

Chris Irvin's B.R.M. is on the side of the track as Jim follows Jo Bonnier's Cooper Maserati at the United States GP at Watkins Glen in 1967. The Lotus cars, despite problems (Clark, suspension, Hill, gear selection), were nursed round the final laps into 1st and 2nd place.

Walter Hayes of Ford is
in the front of this group
as Lotus celebrate 1st
and 2nd place at the
United States GP.

Jim adjusts his helmet as he speaks to Jackie Stewart before the 1967 Mexican GP.

due to lack of fuel. Surtees and Brabham closed right up on him as they entered the Curva Grande for the final time. They swept past him. Jim coasted over the line in third with no fuel left.

It had been an incredible performance. Jim had fluffed the start, pulled his way back into the lead, lost a lap due to tyre problems and then made it up and almost won the race. Perhaps the power of the Lotus 49 was such that Jim's pace was not so surprising, but what was outstanding was his determination. An ordinary driver might have been happy to put in a good performance but a true champion such as Jim knew only one way to drive and that was to win. He would have done it, too, had his fuel pumps been able to siphon out the last three gallons in the tank. Unfortunately some anti-inflammatory foam had been put in the tank along with the fuel and had formed a layer that prevented that last of the fuel from being available to the engine.

Lotus again ran three cars in the US Grand Prix at Watkins Glen. The third car this time was for the Mexican driver Moises Solana. On the first day of practice Jim was quickest but the next day Hill managed beat his time by just over half a second, taking pole with Jim alongside him.

Though not as exciting as Monza, the race had its own share of drama for Lotus. Hill led Jim away from the start, although Jim lost second place for a while to Gurney. He regained it on the eighth lap. The order remained the same, with the Lotus 49s pulling away from the rest of the field, until the forty-fourth lap, when Jim got past Hill's car. Then his car began to develop clutch problems, which plagued him intermittently until the end of the race.

Jim built up a fairly substantial lead over Hill but, with just under three laps to go, the top link in his right-rear suspension broke, meaning that he had to nurse it through the left-hand bends. Jim's lead was over forty-five seconds going into the final two laps but he crossed the finishing line just over six seconds ahead of his team-mate.

This was Jim's third win of the season. He had won more races than any of his rivals but his several retirements were costing him the championship. The 49's reliability was considerably better than his 1966 car's but, going into the final race in Mexico, the championship was between the two Brabham drivers, reigning world champion Jack Brabham and his team-mate and employee Hulme.

'The problem with the Lotus 49 was that I couldn't drive it the way I wanted to. I like to drive deep into a corner with the brakes on, but the back end would flick out mid-corner. It was hell.' — Jim Clark

Again Lotus ran three cars, with Solana in the third car. Jim set the pace in both practice sessions, managing just under 1 minute 49 seconds on the first day and getting it down to 1 minute 47.56 seconds the next. This was despite running in an older chassis, albeit with a new engine. Chris Amon's Ferrari was alongside Jim on the front row, with Gurney behind them. Hill qualified fourth.

Jim again failed to make a smooth getaway from the line and he ended up being hit from behind by Gurney's Eagle-Weslake. Although Jim's exhaust pipe was dented, he came around at the end of the first lap in third place behind Hill and Amon. Within two more laps, he passed them both and took the lead. For sixty-two of the race's sixty-five laps Jim

Graham Hill leads Jim
early in the Mexican GP.
Jim was on majestic form
having taken pole
position and secured
fastest lap, yet again, and
went on to win nearly a
minute and a half ahead
of Jack Brabham.

Jim's last grand prix.
The South African GP at
Kyalami on New Year's
Day 1968. The Lotus
cars finished 1st and
2nd, with Jim once again
starting on pole position
and setting fastest lap
and a course record.
He finished 25 seconds
ahead of team mate
Graham Hill who went
on to win the 1968 World
Champsionship.

(LON-7)JOHANNESBURG STH AFRICA JAN 2(AP)==Jim Clark of Scotland takes the chequered flag after winning the 1968 Grand Prix at Kyalami near Johannesburg yesterday Jan Ist in a Lotus Ford. Clark's speed was a record average of IO7.42 m.p.h. and he set up a track record for the two and a half mile lap of I min 23.I seconds.
(ASSOCIATED PRESS RADIOPHOTO)   lij   arg/aaa   1968.

Taking the chequered flag at Kyalami in South Africa on the 1st January 1968. This was to be Jim's 25th and final world championship victory in Formula 1.

drove with a broken clutch. Despite this, he was able to pull away from the field, such was his ability to adapt his driving style to suit the particular conditions of his car and the circuit at any time. Solana, on the other hand, was driving the Lotus that Jim should have been in and retired after twelve laps with broken suspension.

By lap nineteen Hill was out and by lap twenty Jim's lead was up to twenty-one and a half seconds over Amon. Typically, he got quicker as the race went on, setting a lap record on lap fifty-two, and when he crossed the line he was 1 minute 25 seconds ahead of Brabham. Thus he equalled Juan Manuel Fangio's record of twenty-four wins in grand prix racing. Hulme came in third, which was enough for him to clinch the championship.

Shortly afterwards, Jim won the non-championship grand prix at Jarama, Spain – a country that had been away from FI for a while but was now looking to rejoin the circus. He celebrated with a touch of flamenco.

It had been another disappointing year, but one that was reminiscent of 1962 and 1964. The 49 was obviously the dominant car, though Jim said it was 'quite difficult to drive – much more so than people thought', and the

Right: Jim enjoying himself after the 1967 the Spanish GP – a Formula 2 race organised to demonstrate the viability of the race.

Below: Jim celebrates Christmas Day in South Africa with Colin Chapman on the left and Jack Brabham in the middle.

outlook for 1968 seemed rosy. Although the drivers had equal status, it was likely that Jim would be stronger in the following season and take the title.

According to Jim, 'The problem with the 49 in 1967 was that I couldn't drive the thing the way I wanted to. I like to drive deep into a corner with the brakes on, but whenever I tried to do that with the 49 the back end would flick out mid-corner. It may provide good subject matter for the photographers but it was hell to live with.'

The next year, 1968, was a revolutionary one for motor racing in Europe. For the first time, the F.I.A. allowed sponsorship: Esso had pulled out of supporting motor racing and the teams were very anxious to replace lost income. Fronted by Chapman, Lotus quickly seized the opportunity and the green-and-yellow Lotus colours were soon gone, having one last outing before being replaced by the red colours of the Gold Leaf sponsorship of Imperial Tobacco.

The first grand prix was held on 1 January at Kyalami. The Lotus 49s were essentially the same as in the previous year, although Jim's was newly built for the season. He had a new chief mechanic, too: Bob Dance, who had been with Lotus since 1960. Jim was something of a hero to Bob, the driver he most wanted to work with. Bob was convinced that Lotus would win the constructor's championship in 1968 and Jim the drivers' title.

There were three days of practice, from Thursday to Saturday, with a rest day on Sunday and the race on the Monday. The practice sessions gave rise to yet another demonstration of the awesome alliance of Lotus power and Jim Clark's driving skills. Within four laps of going out on the Thursday, Jim had taken over two seconds off the previous year's lap record, setting a 1 minute 27.6 seconds. He went faster before the end of the session, recording a time of 1 minute 23.9 seconds. This was still in the 43, a completely different beast from the 49. Stewart was within a second of this in the Matra-Cosworth, a car that was so recently put together that it was being run unpainted. Over the next two days Jim went faster again, improving his pole time on both days and getting it down to 1 minute 21.6 seconds. After a more troubled set of practice sessions Hill managed to qualify second and Stewart completed the front row.

Just before the start of the race the temperature was an incredible 130°F, causing the teams to fit extra coolant to the engines. Stewart leaped into the lead, leaving Jim in second place at the end of the first lap. Being Jim, he was already – of course – recovering from this mishap and beginning to put pressure on the Matra, and he passed it before the second lap was completed. From this point in, Jim dominated the race, opening out a lead of a second a lap. Hill passed Stewart on lap twenty-seven but could make no headway on his team-mate. Jim crossed the finishing line twenty-five seconds ahead of Hill, winning his last championship race and setting a new record for F1 victories.

Jim's next motor-racing assignment was the Tasman Series in the southern hemisphere. This was to be the first outing for the new Gold Leaf colours. Judging by the photographs, this time in Australia and New Zealand was not just a period of successful racing but also a relaxing break before the serious business of the FI championship really got going. Jim took part in eight races, retiring from the first two but then winning four out of the next six races, including the Lady Wigram Trophy race in Christchurch, New Zealand. He returned to Europe ready for a little non-championship racing before the FI chase resumed in Spain in May.

Jim driving the 'Gold Leaf' Lotus during the Tasman Series in February 1968 at Surfer's Paradise, Queensland.

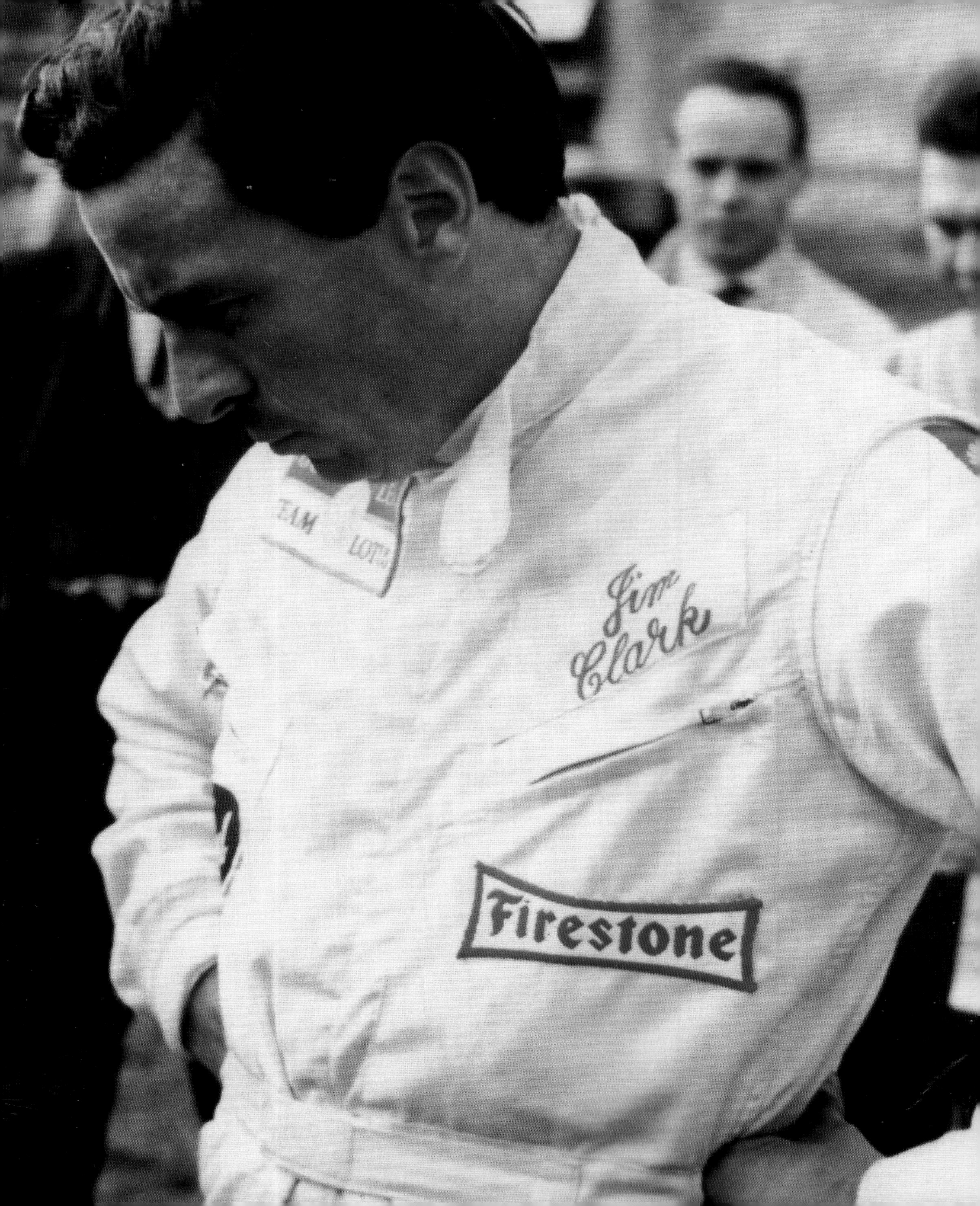
Jim Clark
Firestone

Chapter 6
The Fatal Crash at Hockenheim

FOR FANS OR FRIENDS OF Jim Clark, the word 'Hockenheim' is redolent with sombre connotations. Neither the circuit nor the race organisers did anything to deserve such feelings but Jim's decision to race at Hockenheim that weekend has since caused much regret.

Two weeks earlier, Jim was out in America testing the new Indy 500 car. It was just a normal routine activity. The following week, he raced the Lotus 48 at Barcelona in the opening round of the European Formula 2 Championship. He had a heavy shunt at the start of the race, when Jacky Ickx went into his rear, and the car was heavily damaged. There were only seven days before Hockenheim, so there was no time either to produce a new car or to send the damaged one back to the factory in Hethel. Instead, Lotus's two mechanics had to get it over to Germany and repair it themselves as best they could.

The race at Hockenheim is often described as unimportant and it was in terms of the Formula 1 World Championship, but in the 1960s the top drivers were not confined to just one championship a year. Throughout his career, Jim demonstrated his versatility and his keenness to race anything from milk floats to FI cars. While his FI career was in full flow he was also winning the British Saloon Car Championship and many Formula 2 and GT races in Europe and America. So it was no surprise that Jim was competing at Hockenheim. Graham Hill was there, too, and like Jim he was a former world champion.

Right: Jim speaking to a Lotus mechanic at Hockenheim. He was unhappy with the car's set-up.

Below: One of the last pictures of Jim driving a racing car. A few minutes after this was taken he was dead, having veered off the course and crashed into some trees.

Jim had been offered another drive for that day, in the BOAC 500 at Brands Hatch, a six-hour race for sports cars. Ford wanted him to drive an Alan Mann P65 Ford DFV-engined car. Jim was interested but the commitments for Hockenheim were finalised first. The BOAC 500 might have been a more intriguing prospect for Jim, offering as it did a chance to drive a new car, but only three top drivers were missing from the line-up at Hockenheim – Jackie Stewart, Jacky Ickx and Jackie Oliver – so that was the place to be.

It was always going to be a miserable weekend for Lotus. The weather was awful and the cars were running badly. Jim had never driven at Hockenheim before and was finding the experience dispiriting. Derek Bell, who met Jim that weekend for the only time, later told Eric Dymock, who was researching his biography on Jim, that Jim had no confidence in putting in a good performance in the race. The Lotus was misfiring, the mechanics were unable to put it right and he qualified in seventh place.

The Deutschland Trophy, for which they were competing, was to be held over two heats, with the results of heat one determining the starting grid for heat two. Come the first race, Jim made no impression on the front runners. The car had not improved and he was really only concerned with keeping it going and putting in a respectable finish. On the fifth lap Jim was running on his own in about eighth place when the accident happened. The curve where he came off is described as gentle. It was certainly not a place where a driver would make a misjudgement; the power would be on with the car accelerating up to 160M.P.H.

One of the marshals saw Jim's car shoot off the track at an angle and somersault into the saplings that surrounded the track. Tyre marks on the circuit showed that Jim was fighting it all the way, but to no avail. Nothing available that day could have kept him out of the trees; only a modern barrier could have saved his life. The Lotus hit a tree sideways, suffering massive damage; the gearbox and the engine came apart. Jim's neck was broken, killing him instantly.

News of the accident filtered around the circuit only slowly. First to realise that there might have been a problem was the Lotus pit – they became anxious when Jim's car failed to reappear at the end of the lap. But no one realised immediately that he had had more than a simple breakdown or minor accident. Their first inkling of the truth came when a marshal appeared at the Lotus pit and an ambulance was sent off to the scene of the accident. Graham Hill's car was quietly withdrawn from the race.

Soon after the end of the first heat, an announcement was made to the stunned crowd. Everyone rose to their feet in silent tribute. This was not Jim's first accident but it was the first one in which he was seriously hurt. The race meeting continued: in 1968 there was no feeling that the death of a driver, even one as illustrious as Jim Clark, should halt an event. Driver deaths were not uncommon and it was just part of the event.

The Crash at Hockenheim
'The car seemed to be in a thousand pieces'

Left: Marshals, team mechanics and Lotus team-mate
Graham Hill (second from right) help move the wreckage
from the crash site. Jim was one of more than 100
international drivers killed between 1958 and 1968.

Below: The wrecked remains of Jim's Lotus 48 Formula 2
car at Hockenheim. The extent of the damage shows how
little chance he had of surviving the crash.

Above: Colin Chapman, Jim's mentor and team boss, and
Graham Hill at the scene of Jim's fatal accident at
Hockenheim.

Right: This simple memorial of many years marked the
exact site of the crash. Now that the course has been
redeveloped the memorial has been moved closer to the
new track.

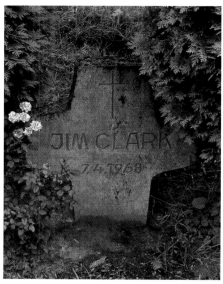

Chapter 7
The Memory

JIM CLARK HAS BEEN DEAD for forty years. Racing in the sixties was a very high-risk occupation, death ever-present. To compete, drivers had to shut the thought of it out of their minds, otherwise they might have been unable to continue driving. When he died, Jim was only a few short weeks past his thirty-second birthday, yet he had achieved so much, including two Formula 1 World Championships, the Indy 500 and the British Saloon Car Championship. Had he lived, he might well have won the championship in 1968, as well: the Lotus 49 was the best car that season and his team-mate Graham Hill went on to become champion. Clark had also won more races than any other driver even though, for much of the time, his car was not a reliable finisher.

It is often said that your local audience is the hardest one to impress, but Jim seems to have retained his sense of proportion. Berwickshire is a thinly populated county in which people seem to know each other intimately; almost everyone would have known someone who knew Jim. He was no ordinary farmer but he did not let it go to his head. In interviews he stressed his ordinariness. In dealings with local people he was very much the Berwickshire man. Before driving in FI he ran the farm – and he stayed involved in its management throughout his career.

Jim's motor racing triumphs were matters for local celebration. The FI World Championships had led to many victory parades through small towns and villages, giving local people an opportunity to see their hero and

hear him speak. There had also been his installation as Duns' first honorary burgess. Jim found all this attention uncomfortable, but he soon learned that it was an expected part of life for a successful international sportsman. As he became more accustomed to the limelight, Jim handled these public duties with greater aplomb, though he never really acted the celebrity role. He did eventually start shopping on Savile Row, for instance, but remained famous for his favourite V-necked sweater, preferring comfort over fashion.

His loss to the motor racing fraternity was one of those J.F.K. moments: people remember where they were.

Jim receiving the inscribed certificate, from Provost Lennie, at his installation as a burgess of Duns. He was the first honorary burgess created in the town's history.

Both Jim's world championship victories in 1963 and 1965 were celebrated enthusiastically by a proud Scottish community. Open-top bus parades and decorated floats sound their way round the villages and towns of East Berwickshire. This shows part of the parade in 1965 at the small village of Allanton, from which it started.

These days, most people can be contacted fairly quickly but this was not the case on 7 April 1968. Ian Scott Watson was at home, working in his study, when he received a phone call from the *Daily Express* in London. Dave Benson, the *Express*'s motor racing correspondent, was at Hockenheim and he rang so that Ian could let Jim's parents know what had happened before it got out onto the television and radio news. Ian's initial reaction was disbelief. Accidents happened but most people had thought nothing serious could happen to Jim. Ian says he 'flunked it' that day, because he was pretty upset himself; instead of ringing Jim's parents he called Alec Calder, Jim's brother-in-law, and let him pass on the news.

Betty Peddie, Jim's sister, remembers that most of the family was away from home and the news took a while to reach them. Jim's parents were out to lunch and someone had to be dispatched to tell them. Betty herself was staying with her parents-in-law.

As the news spread through the racing community and into the wider public, there was a widespread sense of disbelief. Drivers raced because they loved it but they knew that accidents, serious injury and death were possibly just around the next bend. But Jim had seemed indestructible. His mistakes were few and most of his retirements had been for mechani-

'Jimmy was the best driver the world has ever known. His ability was so much greater than he ever revealed. He hardly ever drove to the limits of his capacity.' — Colin Chapman

cal reasons. His death on this seemingly innocent bend was a wake-up call, renewing all thoughts of mortality for his fellow competitors.

Ian was invited to be interviewed on the television news in Carlisle that Sunday evening. He was initially reluctant but decided that it would take his mind off it. When he arrived at the studio he was struck by how glum the Border Television people were, even though they had not known Jim.

Jim's family was left with a trophy collection and other racing equipment from Jim's career and decided to give them to the town of Duns for public display. The arrangement was formalised ten years later with the creation of a trust, the main terms of which underline the strong links that had developed between the family and the local area. Duns Town Council acquired a new base, Westfield House, the former home of the local vet, and renamed one part of it the Jim Clark Memorial Room.

The Room has been open since 1969. Initially the visitors came in vast numbers but it's now a steady stream of about 3,000 a year. Very few are casual visitors looking for something to do. Many are contemporaries of

Jim waves to the crowds with his father on the open-top
bus parade around East Berwickshire in 1965.

Jim's, but many were not even born when he was driving or were just young children, not old enough to have formed any settled opinions about their likes and dislikes. Some visitors come every year, some come for the regular remembrance weekends in May and others to make a solitary pilgrimage to be in the county where their hero grew up.

Eric Bryce, a local farmer, motor racing enthusiast and photographer, met Jim at Charterhall in 1958, having previously photographed him in the Sunbeam Talbot in 1956 or 1957. Jim is often described as shy and a little difficult to talk to but Eric never saw this side of him. Of course, Eric was a farmer, a member of the Berwick and District Motor Club and a keen photographer, all areas of interest to Jim, so the barriers came down quickly.

Eric says that Jim took things in his stride, never giving the impression that he thought he would be a top driver. He never talked about entering 'big-time races'; instead, his mind was very firmly on what he was doing at the time. Jim was greatly interested in motor racing photography and had a large collection of racing photographs from across the world and these provided their main topic of conversation.

Jim always made himself available to people such as Eric, who had a genuine interest in the sport. One thing Eric never experienced, however, was being driven by Jim, either on the road or a on a circuit. George Campbell managed it, however: after one British Grand Prix Jim drove him around Silverstone in the Lotus Elite.

Eric watched Jim race on many occasions, mostly in Scotland but also at the British Grand Prix. In fact, the first time he went to that race was in 1960 at Jim's suggestion. What most impressed him was Jim's smoothness: once he found a line for a corner it would be the same lap and after lap.

He remembers standing at Copse corner during the International Trophy meeting at Silverstone in 1962 taking photographs of the GT race in which Jim was driving the DBR4. It was a wet, miserable day and there were few photographers around. Eric photographed Jim drifting the DBR4 towards the camera for a few laps and then moved away from the corner to get a shot of the car from the side as it pulled out of the corner. On the next lap, the commentator said that Jim Clark had lost it at Copse and was spinning off. Eric looked around to see Jim fighting for control on the grass before rejoining the race.

Afterwards, Jim called Eric over and asked him where he had gone. It turned out that Jim had been using Eric as a marker on the bend; in fact, he had been aiming his car at Eric's head and was momentarily lost when Eric moved away. Why would this have been a problem for a driver of Jim's ability? Eric says it was to do with the nature of the Aston Martin: once you lost it, it was away and it took time to reassert control.

Eric attended every British Grand Prix that Jim drove in, but usually saw only the race, not the practice sessions. In 1967 – Jim's last British

Grand Prix – Eric got away from the farm and attended every practice session. He spent the whole of final practice in the Lotus pit, where he photographed Jim with Graham and Damon Hill in the background. The last photograph that Eric ever took of Jim was with the trophy for that British Grand Prix. Because Jim was a tax exile, Eric never saw him again.

Motorsport has changed a lot since the sixties. Drivers were much more their own bosses in those days. Jim was a bit unusual because most of his later driving was for only one team, but this was due largely to the close friendship that grew between him and Colin Chapman. No doubt Colin was initially keen to have Jim drive for him because of his huge talent. Likewise Jim would have felt flattered that a team owner such as Colin was interested in him, but they developed a bond that was closer than the manager–employee one and Jim's death left Colin in deep shock.

Years later, Colin said he'd long thought that Jim was 'the best driver the world has ever known'. In his analysis, 'His ability was so much greater than he ever revealed. He hardly ever drove to the limits of his capacity.' In other words, if what we saw was good, imagine how much better he'd have seemed if we'd seen him give it his all.

Drivers looked out for each other back then. Hill rescued Stirling Moss from the accident that ended Moss's career and pulled Jackie Stewart out of the wreckage of his B.R.M. at Spa while fuel was spilling onto his clothes.

'My life was hugely enriched by being a friend of Jimmy's and my life has been so much poorer because he left much too soon.' — Jackie Stewart

Danger and death were ever-present and on some of the longer, more dangerous circuits such as Spa and the Nürburgring, where it was impossible to provide enough marshals, the drivers were likely to be the first people on the scene of a major accident, pulling an injured colleague from his car. As a result, they tended to be much closer.

Indeed, Stewart says that 'Jim Clark was the finest racing driver of my era. He was also one of my closest friends' and someone from whom he learned a lot. 'My life was hugely enriched by being a friend of Jimmy's . . . my life has been so much poorer because he left much too soon.'

Jim was 'an incredibly private person,' according to Stewart, who 'hardly confided in anybody'. Even with his closest friends he wouldn't discuss money or the dangers of motorsport. 'He had a stiffness in his shoulders . . . and it got worse as he got older.'

Race Statistics

1956

DATE	FORMULA	LOCATION	EVENT	NO	TYPE	CHASSIS	ENGINE	PLACE	P	FL
Jun 3		Stobs Camp	Sprint over 2,000cc	–	Sunbeam Talbot	–	–	1st	–	–
Jun 16		Crimond	Sports cars under 1,200cc *First actual race*	4	D.K.W.	–	–	8th	–	–
Sep 30		Winfield	Saloons under 1,200cc	–	D.K.W.	–	–	1st	–	–
Sep 30		Winfield	Modified saloons under 1,500cc	–	D.K.W.	–	–	1st	–	–
Sep 30		Winfield	Sprint for saloons unlimited	–	Sunbeam Talbot	–	–	1st	–	–
Sep 30		Winfield	Sprint for modified saloons unlimited	–	Sunbeam Talbot	–	–	1st	–	–
Sep 7		Brunton Beadnell	High speed trials	–	D.K.W.	–	–	6th	–	–
Oct 7		Brunton Beadnell	High speed trials	–	Sunbeam Talbot	–	–	6th	–	–

1957

DATE	FORMULA	LOCATION	EVENT	NO	TYPE	CHASSIS	ENGINE	PLACE	P	FL
Jun 30		Charterhall	Production Cars Handicap	–	D.K.W.	–	–	4th	–	–
Sep 1		Charterhall	Sports cars 1,501–2,700cc	–	Sunbeam Talbot	–	–	8th	–	–
Oct 5		Charterhall	Production sports cars handicap	–	Porsche 1600S	–	–	3rd	–	–
Oct 5		Charterhall	Production touting cars handicap	–	Porsche 1600S	–	–	2nd	–	–
Oct 5		Charterhall	BMRC Trophy *First race win, defeated Jock McBain*	–	Porsche 1600S	–	–	1st	–	–
Oct 6		Winfield	Sprint for modified saloons unlimited *1st equal with Ian Scott Watson*	–	Porsche 1600S	–	–	1st	–	–
Oct 6		Winfield	Sprint for sports cars 1,501–3,000cc	–	Porsche 1600S	–	–	2nd	–	–

1958

DATE	FORMULA	LOCATION	EVENT	NO	TYPE	CHASSIS	ENGINE	PLACE	P	FL
Apr 5		Full Sutton	Racing cars over 500cc	–	Jaguar D-type	–	–	1st	–	–
Apr 5		Full Sutton	Sports cars unlimited *1st average race speed of 100mph per lap*	–	Jaguar D-type	–	–	1st	–	–
Apr 5		Full Sutton	Production sports unlimited	–	Porsche 1600S	–	–	6th	–	–
Apr 20		Winfield	Sprint for saloons under 2,000cc	–	Porsche 1600S	–	–	1st	–	–
Apr 20		Winfield	Sports cars unlimited	–	Porsche 1600S	–	–	2nd	–	–
Apr 27		Charterhall	Racing cars, Formula Libre *Locked brakes*	–	Jaguar D-type	–	–	8th	–	–
Apr 27		Charterhall	Sports cars, 1,501–3,000cc	–	Porsche 1600S	–	–	4th	–	–
Apr 27		Charterhall	Sports cars under 2,000cc *Puncture*	–	Porsche 1600S	–	–	ret	–	–
May 18		Spa-Francochamps	Grand Prix de Spa (over 1,500cc) *1st race abroad*	–	Jaguar D-type	–	–	8th	–	–
May 18		Spa-Francochamps	GT Specials, under 2,000cc	–	Porsche 1600S	–	–	5th	–	–
May 24		Full Sutton	Sports cars unlimited	–	Jaguar D-type	–	–	1st	–	–
May 24		Full Sutton	Formula Libre	–	Jaguar D-type	–	–	1st	–	–

1958

DATE	FORMULA	LOCATION	EVENT	NO	TYPE	CHASSIS	ENGINE	PLACE	P	FL
May 24		Full Sutton	Saloon cars & GT, unlimited	–	Porsche 1600S	–	–	1st	–	–
Jun 8		Stobs Camp	Sprint for sports cars under 2,000cc	–	Porsche 1600S	–	–	1st	–	–
Jun 8		Stobs Camp	Sprint for sports cars under 2,000cc	–	Triumph TR3	–	–	2nd	–	–
Jun 21		Crimond	Sports cars unlimited	–	Jaguar D-type	–	–	1st	–	–
Jun 21		Crimond	Sports cars 1500–3000cc	–	Porsche 1600S	–	–	4th	–	–
Jun 21		Crimond	Invitation Handicap *had to stop to fix undertray*	–	Jaguar D-type	–	–	8th	–	–
Jun 28		Rest-and-Be-Thankful	Production sports cars 1,501–2,000cc *1st hill climb*	–	Porsche 1600S	–	–	1st	–	–
Jun 28		Rest-and-Be-Thankful	Production sports cars 1,501–2,000cc *Hill climb*	–	Triumph TR3	–	–	3rd	–	–
Jun 29		Charterhall	Formula Libre	–	Jaguar D-type	–	–	1st	–	–
Jun 29		Charterhall	Sports cars	–	Jaguar D-type	–	–	1st	–	–
Jul 5		Rest-and-Be-Thankful	Sports cars 1,501–2,000cc	–	Porsche 1600S	–	–	1st	–	–
Jul 5		Rest-and-Be-Thankful	Sports cars 1,501–2,000CC	43	Triumph TR3	–	–	2nd	–	–
Jul 6		Charterhall	Racings cars handicap	–	Jaguar D-type	–	–	1st	–	–
Jul 6		Charterhall	Touring cars handicap	–	Porsche 1600S	–	–	2nd	–	–
Jul 6		Charterhall	Production sports cars	–	Porsche 1600S	–	–	4th	–	–
Jul 6		Charterhall	BMRC Trophy Handicap	–	Jaguar D-type	–	–	2nd	–	–
Jul 12		Full Sutton	Formula Libre	–	Jaguar D-type	–	–	1st	–	–
Jul 12		Full Sutton	Sports cars over 1,500cc	–	Jaguar D-type	–	–	1st	–	–
Jul 12		Full Sutton	Production cars under 1,600cc *Heavy rain*	–	Porsche 1600S	–	–	1st	–	–
Jul 27		Winfield	Sprint for touring cars mod. over 1,500cc	–	Porsche 1600S	–	–	1st	–	–
Jul 27		Winfield	Sprint for sports cars 1,501–3,000cc	–	Porsche 1600S	–	–	1st	–	–
Jul 27		Winfield	Sprint for sports and racing cars unlimited	–	Jaguar D-type	–	–	1st	–	–
Aug 4		Mallory Park	Sports cars over 1,500cc	–	Jaguar D-type	–	–	1st	–	–
Aug 4		Mallory Park	Formula Libre heat	–	Jaguar D-type	–	–	2nd	–	–
Aug 4		Mallory Park	Formula Libre final	–	Jaguar D-type	–	–	7th	–	–
Aug 16		Silverstone	6-hour relay race handicap	–	Porsche 1600S	–	–	22nd	–	–
Sep 28		Charterhall	Formula Libre	–	Jaguar D-type	–	–	2nd	–	–
Sep 28		Charterhall	Sports cars over 1,500cc	–	Jaguar D-type	–	–	3rd	–	–
Sep 28		Charterhall	Production sports cars under 1600cc	–	Porsche 1600S	–	–	3rd	–	–
Dec 26		Brands Hatch	GT cars unlimited cc *Colin Chapman won race after passing J.C. near the end with the help of a car that was being lapped*	–	Lotus Elite	–	–	2nd	–	–

1959

DATE	FORMULA	LOCATION	EVENT	NO	TYPE	CHASSIS	ENGINE	PLACE	P	FL
Mar 30		Mallory Park	GT cars 1,000–1,600cc	–	Lotus Elite	–	–	1st	–	–
Mar 30		Mallory Park	Sports cars over 1,200cc	–	Lister-Jaguar	–	–	1st	–	–
Apr 11		Oulton Park	Sports cars under 1,500cc	–	Lotus Elite	–	–	10th	–	–
Apr 11		Oulton Park	Sports cars over 1,500cc	–	Lister-Jaguar	–	–	8th	–	–
Apr 18		Aintree	Sports cars over 1,500cc	–	Lister-Jaguar	–	–	6th	–	–
Apr 25		Charterhall	Sports cars over 2,000cc	–	Lister-Jaguar	–	–	1st	–	–
Apr 25		Charterhall	Formula Libre	–	Lister-Jaguar	–	–	1st	–	–
Apr 25		Charterhall	GT under 1600cc	–	Porsche 1600S	–	–	2nd	–	–
May 18		Goodwood	Whitsun Trophy, sports cars *Ran out of fuel*	–	Lister-Jaguar	–	–	Ret	–	–
May 30		Rufforth	Sports cars, unlimited cc	–	Lister-Jaguar	–	–	1st	–	–
May 30		Rufforth	Formula Libre	–	Lister-Jaguar	–	–	2nd	–	–
Jun 7		Stobs Camp	Sprint for GT cars under 1,600cc	–	Porsche 1600S	–	–	1st	–	–
Jun 7		Stobs Camp	Sprint for sports cars unlimited CC & FTD	–	Porsche 1600S	–	–	1st	–	–
Jun 20–21		Le Mans	Index *Co-driver: John Whitmore, Border Reivers. Starter motor problems*	42	Lotus Elite MK 14	–	–	11th	–	–
Jul 5		Zandvoort	GT World Cup Race *Rear axle*	–	Lotus Elite		ret	–	–	

1959

DATE	FORMULA	LOCATION	EVENT	NO	TYPE	CHASSIS	ENGINE	PLACE	P	FL
Jul 11		Bo'ness Hill Climb	Sports cars over 2,000cc *Record time for sports car*	–	Lister-Jaguar	–	–	1st	–	–
Jul 11		Bo'ness Hill Climb	Sports cars under 1,600cc	–	Lotus Elite	–	–	1st	–	–
Jul 11		Bo'ness Hill Climb	Sports cars under 1,600cc	25	Porsche 1600S	–	–	7th	–	–
Jul 18		Aintree	Sports cars over 2,000cc	24	Lister-Jaguar	–	–	2nd	–	–
Jul 26		Winfield	Sprint for sports cars over 1,500cc	–	Lister-Jaguar	–	–	1st	–	–
Jul 26		Winfield	Sprint for for GT cars 1,000–2,000cc	–	Lotus Elite	–	–	1st	–	–
Jul 26		Winfield	Sprint for for GT cars 1,000–2,000cc	–	Porsche 1600S	–	–	2nd	–	–
Jul 26		Winfield	Formula Libre & FTD	–	Lister-Jaguar	–	–	1st	–	–
Aug 2		Mallory Park	Formula Libre Heat	–	Lister-Jaguar	–	–	3rd	–	–
Aug 2		Mallory Park	Formula Libre Final	–	Lister-Jaguar	–	–	4th	–	–
Aug 2		Mallory Park	Sports cars over 1,200cc heat	–	Lister-Jaguar	–	–	2nd	–	–
Aug 2		Mallory Park	Sports cars over 1,200cc final	–	Lister-Jaguar	–	–	2nd	–	–
Aug 2		Mallory Park	GT cars up to 1,600cc *Had to replace plug*	–	Lotus Elite	–	–	2nd	–	–
Aug 18		Goodwood	Tourist Trophy *Ecurie Écosse with Masten Gregory who crashed*	–	Tojeiro-Jaguar	–	–	ret	–	–
Aug 29		Brands Hatch	World Cup Race heat 1	–	Lotus Elite	–	–	1st	–	–
Aug 29		Brands Hatch	World cup Race heat 2	–	Lotus Elite	–	–	2nd	–	–
Aug 29		Brands Hatch	Sports cars over 3,000cc	–	Lister-Jaguar	–	–	1st	–	–
Sep 13		Mallory Park	Sports cars over 1,200cc	–	Lister-Jaguar	–	–	1st	–	–
Sep 13		Mallory Park	Formula Libre, heat	–	Lister-Jaguar	–	–	3rd	–	–
Sep 13		Mallory Park	Formula Libre, final	–	Lister-Jaguar	–	–	8th	–	–
Sep 13		Mallory Park	GT 1000–1600cc	–	Lotus Elite	–	–	1st	–	–
Sep 26		Oulton Park	GT cars under 1,600cc	–	Lotus Elite	–	–	1st	–	–
Sep 27		Charterhall	Sports cars over 1,500cc *Dropped valve*	–	Lister-Jaguar	–	–	ret	–	–
Sep 27		Charterhall	Sports cars under 1,300cc	–	Lotus Elite	–	–	5th	–	–
Sep 27		Charterhall	GT cars unlimited cc	–	Lotus Elite	–	–	1st	–	–
Oct 4		Charterhall	Sports cars over 1,500cc	–	Lister-Jaguar	–	–	1st	–	–
Oct 4		Charterhall	Formula Libre	–	Lister-Jaguar	–	–	1st	–	–
Oct 4		Charterhall	GT cars unlimited cc	–	Lotus Elite	–	–	1st	–	–
Oct 4		Charterhall	Sports cars under 1,300cc	–	Lotus Elite	–	–	4th	–	–
Oct 4		Charterhall	BMRC Trophy Handicap	–	Lister-Jaguar	–	–	13th	–	–
Oct 10		Snetterton	Autosport 3-hour	–	Lotus Elite	–	–	1st	–	–
Dec 26		Brands Hatch	GT cars unlimited cc *Crashed*	–	Lotus Elite	–	–	Ret	–	–
Dec 26		Brands Hatch	Formula Junior	–	Gemini	–	–	Ret	–	–

1960 – *10th in Driver's Championships: 8 points; winner Jack Brabham: 43 points*

DATE	FORMULA	LOCATION	EVENT	NO	TYPE	CHASSIS	ENGINE	PLACE	P	FL
Mar 19	FJ	Goodwood	Formula Junior *First race for Lotus*	–	Lotus 18	–	Cosworth-Ford	1st	–	FL
Apr 2	FJ	Oulton Park	Formula Junior	–	Lotus 18	–	Cosworth-Ford	1st	–	FL
Apr 2		Oulton Park	Sports Cars *Border Reivers*	–	Aston Martin DBR1	–	–	3rd	–	–
Apr 10	F2	Brussels	Brussels GP	6	Lotus 18	–	Climax	ret	–	–
Apr 16	FJ	Goodwood	Formula Junior	–	Lotus 18	–	Climax	1st	–	FL
Apr 16		Goodwood	Sports cars *Border Reivers*	–	Aston Martin DBR1	–	–	ret	–	–
Apr 30	F2	Aintree	BARC '200' *Shared car with Innes Ireland*	3	Lotus 18	–	Cosworth-Ford	9th	–	–
May 14	FJ	Silverstone	Formula Junior	–	Lotus 18 FJ	–	Cosworth-Ford	1st	–	–
		Silverstone	Sports cars *Border Reivers, throttle linkage*	–	Aston Martin DBR1	–	–	ret	–	–
May 22		Nürburgring	1,000KM Race *Shared car with Roy Salvadori, Border Reivers; broken crank*	11	Aston Martin DBR1	–	–	ret	–	–

1960

DATE	FORMULA	LOCATION	EVENT	NO	TYPE	CHASSIS	ENGINE	PLACE	P	FL
May 29	FJ	Monaco	Formula Junior *Ignition lead broke while in the lead*	–	Lotus 18	–	Cosworth-Ford	7th	–	–
Jun 6	FI/WC	Zandvoort	Dutch GP *Retired from 3rd place with transmission problems*	6	Lotus 18	–	Climax	ret	–	–
Jun 20-21		Le Mans	24-hour race *Co-driver Roy Salvadori, Border Reivers*	38	Aston-Martin DBRI/300			3rd	–	–
Jun 19	FI/WC	Spa-Francorchamps	Belgian GP	–	Lotus 18	–	Climax	5th	–	–
Jul 3	FI/WC	Reims	French GP	–	Lotus 18	–	Climax	5th	–	–
Jul 16	FI/WC	Silverstone	British GP	8	Lotus 18	–	Climax	16th	–	–
Jul 24	F2	Solitude	South German GP	–	Lotus 18	–	Climax	8th	–	–
	FJ	Solitude	Formula Junior	–	Lotus 18	–	Cosworth-Ford	1st	–	FL
Aug 1		Brands Hatch	Silver City Trophy *While in 2nd place with transmission problems*	34	Lotus 18	374	Climax	ret	P	–
	FJ	Brands Hatch	Formula Junior	47	Lotus 18	–	Cosworth-Ford	1st	P	FL
Aug 14	FI/WC	Boavista	Portuguese GP *Car almost completely rebuilt after final practice*	14	Lotus 18	–	Climax	3rd	–	–
Aug 19	FJ	Goodwood	BARC Formula Junior Championship	–	Lotus 18	–	Cosworth-Ford	2nd	–	FL
Aug 28	F2	Brands Hatch	Kentish '100'	48	Lotus 18	–	Climax	2nd	–	–
	FJ	Brands Hatch	Formula Junior Race *Spun off circuit during race*	–	Lotus 18	–	–	2nd	–	–
Sep 17	FI/NC	Snetterton	Lombank Trophy	8	Lotus 18	372	Climax	2nd	–	FL
	FJ	Snetterton	Formula Junior	–	Lotus 18			1st	–	–
Sep 24	FI/NC	Oulton Park	International Gold Cup *Crashed with Naylor*	5	Lotus 18	374	Climax	ret	–	FL
	FJ	Oulton Park	Formula Junior heat 1	–	Lotus 18	–	Cosworth-Ford	1st	–	–
	FJ	Oulton Park	Formula Junior heat 2	–	Lotus 18	–	Cosworth-Ford	1st	–	–
Sep 25	FJ	Charterhall	Formula Libre *Last race in Scotland, started at back of the grid as he did not take part in practice. Only time he drove a single-seater in Scotland*	39	Lotus 18	–	–	ret	–	–
Nov 20	FI/WC	Riverside	United States GP *Crashed with John Surtees*	–	Lotus 18	–	Climax	16th	–	–
Dec 26	FJ	Brands Hatch	John Davy Trophy *Last Formula Junior race*	–	Lotus 18	–	Cosworth-Ford	1st	–	–

1961 – *7th in Driver's Championships: 11 points; winner Phil Hill: 34 points*

DATE	FORMULA	LOCATION	EVENT	NO	TYPE	CHASSIS	ENGINE	PLACE	P	FL
Jan 7		Ardmore	New Zealand GP *Tasman Series*	–	Lotus 18 I-C	–	Climax	6th	–	–
Jan 14		Levin	Inter-Continental Race *Tasman Series*	–	Lotus 18 I-C	–	Climax	2nd	–	–
Jan 21		Christchurch	Lady Wigram Trophy *Tasman Series, spun off*	–	Lotus 18 I-C	–	Climax	ret	–	–
Mar 26		Shetterton	Lombank Trophy	7	Lotus	–	Climax	6th	–	–
Apr 3	FI/NC	Pau	Pau GP *First win in a Grand Prix race*	6	Lotus 18	–	Climax	1st	–	FL
Apr 8	FI/NC	Brussels	Brussels GP *From 4th place with gear box problems*	22	Lotus 18	374	Climax	ret	–	–
Apr 22	FI/NC	Aintree	Aintree 200	19	Lotus 18	372	Climax	9th	–	–
Apr 26	FI/NC	Syracuse	Syracuse GP	20	Lotus 18	374	–	6th	–	–
May 6		Silverstone	Daily Express Trophy	–	Lotus 18	–	–	8th	–	–
May 14	FI/WC	Monte Carlo	Monaco GP *Ignition lead came loose*	–	Lotus 21	–	Climax	10th	–	–
May 22	FI/WC	Zandvoort	Dutch GP	15	Lotus 21	–	Climax	3rd	–	FL
May 28		Nürburgring	1,000KM Race *Co-driver Bruce McLaren, engine problems*	–	Aston Martin DBRI	–	–	ret	–	–
Jun 3		Brands Hatch	Silver City Trophy	24	Lotus 21	930	Climax	2nd	–	–
Jun 9		Le Mans	24-hour race *Co-driver Ron Flockhart, Border Reivers, clutch problems*	–	Aston Martin DBRI	–	–	ret	–	–
Jun 18	FI/WC	Spa-Francorchamps	Belgian GP	–	Lotus 21	–	Climax	12th	–	FL
Jul 2	FI/WC	Reims	French GP	–	Lotus 21	–	Climax	3rd	–	–

1961

DATE	FORMULA	LOCATION	EVENT	NO	TYPE	CHASSIS	ENGINE	PLACE	P	FL
Jul 9		Silverstone	British Empire Trophy	–	Lotus 18	–	–	5th	–	–
Jul 15	F1/WC	Aintree	British GP *Oil pipe when in 4th place*	–	Lotus 21	–	Climax	ret	–	–
Jul 23		Stuttgart	Solitude GP	2	Lotus 21	932	Climax	7th	–	–
Aug 6	F1	Nürburgring	German GP *Drove spare car after steering failure in practice*	–	Lotus 21	–	Climax	4th	–	–
Aug 7		Brands Hatch	Guards Trophy	–	Lotus 18	–	Climax	2nd	–	–
Aug 19		Goodwood	Tourist Trophy	–	Aston Martin DB4	–	–	4th	–	–
Aug 20		Karlskoga	Swedish GP *Suspension/oil tank*	10	Lotus 21	930	Climax	ret	P	–
Aug 27		Roskildering	Danish GP *Steering problems*	4	Lotus 18	371	Climax	4th	–	–
Sep 3		Modena	Modena GP *Had only two functioning gears at finish*	14	Lotus 21	933	Climax	4th	–	–
Sep 10	F1/WC	Monza	Italian GP *Accident – von Tripps killed*	–	Lotus 21	–	Climax	ret	–	–
Sep 17		Zeltweg	Austrian GP *After three steering failures*	5	Lotus 21	930	Climax	4th	–	–
Sep 23		Oulton Park	Gold Cup race *Rear suspension*	5	Lotus 21	930	Climax	ret	–	–
Sep 24		Charterhall	Formula Libre *Border Reivers*	–	Aston Martin DBR1	–	–	2nd	–	–
		Charterhall	Sports cars unlimited *Border Reivers, last race in Scotland*	–	Aston Martin DBR1	–	–	2nd	–	–
Oct 15		Montlhery	Paris 100KM race *Co-driver Innes Ireland*	–	Aston Martin DB4	–	–	6th	–	–
Oct 8	F1/WC	Watkins Glen	United States GP	–	Lotus 21	–	Climax	7th	–	–
Dec 9		Kyalami	Rand GP	1	Lotus 21	937	Climax	1st	P	–
Dec 17		Westmead, Durban	Natal GP	8	Lotus 21	937	Climax	1st	P	–
Dec 26		East London	South African GP	1	Lotus 21	937	Climax	1st	P	FL

1962 – *2nd in world championship: 30 points; winner Graham Hill: 42 points*

DATE	FORMULA	LOCATION	EVENT	NO	TYPE	CHASSIS	ENGINE	PLACE	P	FL
Jan 1		Cape Town	Cape GP	1	Lotus 21	933	Climax	2nd	P	FL
Feb 11		Daytona	Inter-Continental GT Race 1,300cc *Battery failure while in the lead*	–	Lotus Elite	–	–	4th	–	–
Mar 12		Sandown	Formula Libre heat *Tasman Series*	–	Lotus 21/2,500cc	–	Climax	2nd	–	–
			Formula Libre final	–	Lotus 21/2,500cc	–	Climax	6th	–	–
Apr 1		Brussels	Brussels GP *Valve*	6	Lotus 24	948	Climax	ret	P	–
Apr 14		Snetterton	Lombank Trophy	3	Lotus 24	948	Climax	1st	–	–
Apr 23		Pau	Pau GP *Gear selection*	2	Lotus 24	948	Climax	ret	P	FL
Apr 29		Aintree	Aintree 200	5	Lotus 24	948	Climax V8	1st	P	FL
May 12		Silverstone	BRDC International Trophy sports car race	11	Lotus 24 Aston-Martin DBR1	948	Climax V8	2nd 3rd	– –	FL –
May 20	F1/WC	Zandvoort	Dutch GP *Clutch problems*	4	Lotus 25	–	Climax V8	9th	–	–
May 27		Nürburgring	1,000KM race *Crashed while leading*	82	Lotus 23	–	Ford T/C	ret	–	–
Jun 3	F1/WC	Monte Carlo	Monaco GP *Lap 55, clutch problems*	–	Lotus 25	–	Climax V8	ret	P	FL
Jun 11	F1/NC	Mallory Park	2,000 Guineas Race *Oil pressure*	6	Lotus 25	R1	Climax V8	ret	P	–
Jun 17	F1/WC	Spa-Francorchamps	Belgian GP *Qualified 12th & 1st Championship GP win*	16	Lotus 25	–	Climax V8	1st	–	FL

1962

DATE	FORMULA	LOCATION	EVENT	NO	TYPE	CHASSIS	ENGINE	PLACE	P	FL
Jul 1	F1/NC	Rheims	Rheims GP *Oveheating engine*	10	Lotus 25	R1	Climax v8	ret	P	–
Jul 8	F1/WC	Rouen-les-Essarts	French GP *Lap 33, suspension*	12	Lotus 25	–	Climax v8	ret	P	–
Jul 15	F1/NC	Stuttgart	Solitude GP *Suspension/crash*	1	Lotus 25	R2	Climax v8	ret	P	–
Jul 21	F1/WC	Aintree	British GP *First win in home GP*	20	Lotus 25	–	Climax v8	1st	P	FL
Aug 5	F1/WC	Nürburgring	German GP *Stalled on start line*	5	Lotus 25	–	Climax v8	4th	–	–
Aug 6		Brands Hatch	Guards Trophy *Clutch problems*	–	Lotus 23	–	Ford T/C	ret	–	–
Aug 18		Goodwood	Tourist Trophy *Crash*	2	Aston-Martin DB4	–	–	ret	–	–
Aug 26		Ollon-Villars	Hill Climb	–	Lotus 21	–	Climax	3rd	–	–
Sep 1		Oulton Park	Sports car race	–	Lotus 23	–	Ford T/C	2nd	–	–
	F1/WC		International Gold Cup	8	Lotus 25	R2	Climax v8	1st	–	FL
Sep 16	F1/WC	Monza	Italian GP *Lap 12, transmission*	–	Lotus 25	–	Climax v8	ret	P	–
Sep 29		Snetterton	3-hour race	–	Lotus 23	–	Ford T/C	1st	–	–
Oct 7	F1/WC	Watkins Glen	United States GP	8	Lotus 25	–	Climax v8	1st	P	FL
Oct 21		Montlhery	Paris 100KM race *Co-driver John Whitmore, piston*	–	Aston-Martin DB4	–	–	ret	–	–
Nov 4	F1/NC	Mexico City	Mexican GP *In Trevor Taylor's car/push start*	29	Lotus 25	R3	Climax v8	1st	P	FL
Dec 15	F1/NC	Kyalami	Rand GP	1	Lotus 25	R3	Climax v8	1st	P	FL
Dec 22	F1/NC	Westmead, Durban	Natal GP, Heat *Fuel injection*	1	Lotus 25	R4	Climax v8	2nd	–	–
Dec 29	F1/WC	East London	South African GP *Championship decider. JC 1st on grid but ret on lap 61, gave ch'ship to Graham Hill and leading but championsip went to Graham Hill*	–	Lotus 25	R4	Climax v8	ret	P	–

1963 – *World champion: 54 world championship points, 73 points in all*

DATE	FORMULA	LOCATION	EVENT	NO	TYPE	CHASSIS	ENGINE	PLACE	P	FL
Mar 30	F1/NC	Snetterton	Lombank Trophy	3	Lotus 25	R3	Climax v8	2nd	P	–
Apr 6		Oulton Park	British Empire Trophy	–	Lotus 23	–	Climax v8	1st	–	–
Apr 15	F1/NC	Pau	Pau GP	2	Lotus 25	R5	Climax v8	1st	P	FL
Apr 21	F1/NC	Imola	Imola GP	4	Lotus 25	–	Climax v8	1st	P	–
Apr 27	F1/NC	Aintree	BARC Aintree '200' *In Trevor Taylor's car due to battery failure*	3	Lotus 25	R5	Climax v8	7th	P	FL
May 11	F1/NC	Silverstone	BRDC International Trophy	3	Lotus 25	R5	Climax v8	1st	–	–
May 26	F1/WC	Monte Carlo	Monaco GP *Retired lap 68 with gearbox seizure*	9	Lotus 25	R4	Climax v8	8th	P	–
May 30	INDY CAR	Indianapolis	Indy 500 *Denied chance of victory because of oil leak*	92	Lotus 29	–	Ford	2nd	–	–
Jun 1		Mossport	Sports car race	–	Lotus 23	–	Ford T/C	3rd	–	–
Jun 3		Crystal Palace	Sports car race	–	Lotus 23	–	–	1st	–	–
Jun 9	F1/WC	Spa-Francochamps	Belgian GP *Led from start to finish despite being 8th on the grid*	1	Lotus 25	R4	Climax v8	1st	–	FL
Jun 23	F1/WC	Zandvoort	Dutch GP *Pole and led from start of race*	6	Lotus 25	R4	Climax v8	1st	P	FL
Jun 30	F1/WC	Reims	French GP *Led from start of race*	–	Lotus 25	R4	Climax v8	1st	P	FL
Jul 20	F1/WC	Silverstone	British GP	4	Lotus 25	R4	Climax v8	1st	P	–
Jul 28	F1/NC	Stuttgart	Solitude GP *Drive shaft/crash*	–	Lotus 25	R4	Climax v8	RET	P	FL
Aug 4	F1/WC	Nürburgring	German GP *Pole but had engine problems*	3	Lotus 25	R4	Climax v8	2nd	P	–

1963

DATE	FORMULA	LOCATION	EVENT	NO	TYPE	CHASSIS	ENGINE	PLACE	P	FL
Aug 5		Brands Hatch	Saloon car race	–	Ford Galaxy	R3	–	1st	–	–
Aug 11	F1/NC	Karlskoga	Swedish GP	3	Lotus 25	–	Climax v8	1st	–	FL
Aug 18		Milwaukee	Milwaukee '200'	–	Lotus 29	–	Ford	1st	–	–
Sep 1	F1/NC	Zeltweg	Austrian GP *Oil pipe*	2	Lotus 25	R6	Climax v8	ret	P	–
Sep 8	F1/WC	Monza	Italian GP *Clinched world championship*	8	Lotus 25	R4	Climax v8	1st	P	–
Sep 21	F1/NC	Oulton Park	Gold Cup	4	Lotus 25	R4	Climax v8	1st	P	FL
			Sports car race	–	Lotus 23			1st	–	–
Sep 22		Trenton	State Fair race *Oil leak while leading*	–	Lotus 29	–	Ford	ret	–	–
Sep 28		Snetterton	Three Hours Race	–	Lotus 23	–	Ford T/C	1st	–	–
			Touring cars	–	Lotus Cortina		Ford T/C	1st	–	–
Oct 6	F1/WC	Watkins Glen	USGP *Left behind on dummy grid due to battery problems*	–	Lotus 25	R4	Climax v8	3rd	–	FL
Oct 13		Riverside	Riverside GP	–	Lotus 23	–	Ford T/C	1st	–	–
Oct 20		Laguna Seca	Monterey GP *Oil cooler*	–	Lotus 19	–	Climax	ret	–	–
Oct 27	F1/WC	Mexico City	Mexican GP *Led from pole*	–	Lotus 25	R4	Climax v8	1st	P	FL
Dec 14	F1	Kyalami	Rand GP *Fuel pump*	–	Lotus 25	R4	Climax v8	ret	–	–
Dec 28	F1/WC	East London	South African GP	1	Lotus 25	–	Climax v8	1st	P	–

1964 – *3rd in Driver's Championship: 32 points; winner John Surtees: 40 points*

DATE	FORMULA	LOCATION	EVENT	NO	TYPE	CHASSIS	ENGINE	PLACE	P	FL
Mar 14	F1/NC	Snetterton	Daily Mirror Trophy *Lap 30, ignition problems*	1	Lotus 25	R6	Climax v8	ret	P	–
Mar 14	Saloon car	Snetterton	Saloon car race *(1st in class)*	71	Lotus Cortina	–	Ford T/C	2nd	–	–
Mar 22		Sebring	Saloon car race *(1st in class)*	–	Lotus Cortina	–	Ford T/C	3rd	–	–
Mar 23		Sebring	12-hours race *(2nd in class)*	–	Lotus Cortina	–	Ford T/C	21st	–	–
Mar 30	F1/NC	Goodwood	News of the World Trophy	1	Lotus 25	R6	Climax v8	1st	–	–
Mar 30	Saloon car	Goodwood	Saloon car race *(1st in class)*	95	Lotus Cortina		Ford T/C	2nd	–	FL
Mar 30	Sports car	Goodwood	Lavant Cup	–	Lotus 19	–	Climax	1st	–	–
Apr 5	F2	Pau	Pau GP	4	Lotus 32	–	Cosworth SCA	1st	–	–
Apr 11	Sports car	Oulton Park	Oulton Park Trophy *Entered in type 30 but car not ready in time*	–	Lotus 19	–	Climax	1st	–	–
Apr 11	Saloon car	Oulton Park	Saloon car race	45	Lotus Cortina	–	Ford T/C	3rd	–	–
Apr 11			GT Cars	–	Lotus Elan	–	Ford T/C	1st	–	–
Apr 18	F1/F2	Aintree	BARC '200' *Crashed*	1	Lotus 33	R8	Climax v8	ret	–	FL
Apr 18	Sports car	Aintree	BARC sports car race	82	30	–	Ford v8	2nd	–	FL
Apr 18	Saloon car	Aintree	BARC saloon car race *(1st in class)*	–	Lotus Cortina	–	Ford T/C	3rd	–	FL
Apr 26	F2	Nürburgring	Eifel F2 Race	–	Lotus 32	–	Cosworth SCA	1st	P	FL
May 2	F1/NC	Silverstone	BRDC International *blown engine on lap 10*	1	Lotus 25	R6	Climax	ret	–	–
May 2	Saloon car	Silverstone	Saloon car race *(1st class)*	21	Lotus Cortina	–	Ford T/C	3rd	–	FL
May 2	GT	Silverstone	GT race *(class)*	–	Lotus Elan	–	Ford T/C	1st	–	FL
			Sports cars	–	Lotus 30	–	Ford	ret	–	–
May 10	F1/WC	Monte Carlo	Monaco GP *Retired with engine problems on lap 96*	–	Lotus 25	–	Climax v8	4th	P	–
May 16	F2	Mallory Park	Grovewood Trophy	–	Lotus 32	–	Cosworth SCA	1st	P	FL
May 16	Sports Car	Mallory Park	Sport Cars	–	Lotus 30	–	Ford	1st	P	FL

1964

DATE	FORMULA	LOCATION	EVENT	NO	TYPE	CHASSIS	ENGINE	PLACE	P	FL
May 16	Sports car	Mallory Park	Guards Trophy	43	Lotus 30	–	Ford T/C	1st	–	–
May 18	F2	Crystal Palace	London Trophy *Heat 1 2nd, Final, 10th*	1	Lotus 32	–	Climax			
May 18	Saloon car	Crystal Palace	London LT meeting	57	Lotus Cortina	–	Cosworth SCA	1st	–	–
May 24	FI/WC	Zandvoort	Dutch GP *Led from start*	–	Lotus 25	–	Climax V8	1st	–	FL
May 30	Indy 500	Indianapolis	Indianapolis 500 *Start first, fastest time, led for 14 of 27 laps completed*	6	Lotus		Ford 4-CAM	ret	–	–
Jun 14	FI/WC	Spa-Francorchamps	Belgian GP *Ran out of fuel over the line*	23	Lotus 25	–	Climax V8	1st	–	–
Jun 28	FI/WC	Rouen-les-Essarts	French GP	–	Lotus 25	–	Climax V8	ret	P	–
Jul 5	F2	Rheims	Rheims GP	–	Lotus 32	–	Cosworth SCA	4th	–	–
Jul 11	FI/WC	Brands Hatch	European GP *Led from pole to the finish*	1	Lotus 33	–	Climax V8	1st	P	FL
Jul 19	FI/NC	Stuttgart	Solitude GP *Rained heavily*	6	Lotus 33	R8	Climax V8	1st	P	FL
Aug 2	FI/WC	Nürburgring	German GP *Lap 7, engine problems*	–	Lotus 33	–	Climax V8	ret	–	–
Aug 3	F2	Brands Hatch	British Eagle Trophy	48	Lotus 32	–	Cosworth SCA	1st	–	–
Aug 3	Sports car	Brands Hatch	Guards International Trophy *Water hose*	–	Lotus 30	–	Ford V8	ret	–	–
Aug 3	Saloon car	Brands Hatch	Saloon car race *(1st class)*	68	Lotus Cortina		Ford T/C	2nd	–	–
Aug 9	F2	Karlskoga	Canon F2 race	–	Lotus 32	–	Cosworth SCA	2nd	–	–
Aug 16	FI	Enna–Pergusa	Mediterranean GP	10	Lotus 25	R6	Climax V8	2nd	–	–
Aug 23	FI/WC	Zeltweg	Austrian GP *Lap 40, drive shaft*	1	Lotus 33	–	Climax V8	ret	–	–
Aug 29	Sports car	Goodwood	RAC Tourist Trophy *Fourth in class*	1	30	–	Ford V8	12th	–	–
Sep 6	GP	Monza	Italian GP *Lap 27, engine*	–	Lotus 33	–	Climax V8	15th	–	–
Sep 13	F2	Albi	Albi GP	–	Lotus 32	–	Cosworth SCA	ret	–	–
Sep 19	F2	Oulton Park	Gold Cup	1	32	–	Cosworth SCA	2nd	–	FL
Sep 19	Saloon car	Oulton Park	Saloon car race	–	Lotus Cortina	–	Ford T/C	1st	–	FL
Sep 26		Mosport	Sports cars	–	Lotus 30	–	Ford V8	ret	–	–
Sep 27		Trenton	USAC race	–	Lotus 34	–	Ford 4-CAM	ret	–	–
Oct 4	FI/WC	Watkins Glen	USGP *Switched cars with Mike Spence which meant he could not score points*	–	Lotus 33	–	Climax V8	7th	P	FL
Oct 11		Riverside	Sports cars	–	Lotus 30	–	Ford V8	3rd	–	–
Oct 25	FI/WC	Mexico City	Mexican GP *Engine seized on lap 64 of a 65 lap race, lost title as a result*	–	Lotus 33	–	Climax V8	5th	P	FL

1965 – *World champion: 54 points*

DATE	FORMULA	LOCATION	EVENT	NO	TYPE	CHASSIS	ENGINE	PLACE	P	FL
Jan 1	FI/WC	East London	South African GP *Pole, start to finish win*	–	Lotus 33	–	Climax V8	1st	P	FL
Jan 1	FI/WC	East London	South African GP *Pole, start to finish win*	–	Lotus 33	–	Climax V8	1st	–	–
Jan 16		Levin	Tasman Cup *Won heat & final* Flying Farewell	– –	Lotus 32 Lotus 32	– –	Climax V8 Climax V8	1st 1st	P P	FL FL
Jan 23		Christchurch	Lady Wigram Trophy *Won both heat & final*	–	Lotus 32	–	Climax V8	1st	P	–
Jan 30		Invercargill	Teretonga Trophy *Won heat & final* Flying Farewell	– –	Lotus 32 Lotus 32	– –	Climax V8 Climax V8	1st 2nd	P –	FL –
Feb 14		Warwick Farm	Tasman Cup	–	Lotus 32	–	Climax V8	1st	–	FL
Feb 21		Sandown Park	Tasman Cup	–	Lotus 32	–	Climax V8	2nd	–	–

1965

DATE	FORMULA	LOCATION	EVENT	NO	TYPE	CHASSIS	ENGINE	PLACE	P	FL
Mar 1		Longford	Tasman Cup *5th in both heat & final*	–	Lotus 32	–	Climax	5th	–	–
Mar 7		Lakeside	Tasman Cup	1	Lotus 32	–	Climax	1st	–	–
Mar 13	F1/NC	Brands Hatch	Race of Champions *Heat 1 1st, heat 2 ret (crashed)*	5	Lotus 33	R10	Climax v8		P	FL
Mar 13	Saloon car	Brands Hatch	Saloon car race *Broken wheel*	–	Lotus Cortina	–	Ford T/C	ret	–	–
Mar 20	F2	Silverstone	BARC Senior Service Trophy *Race abandoned – waterlogged track – in 2nd place*	19	Lotus 35	–	Cosworth SCA	DNF		
Mar 20	Sports car	Silverstone	Guards Trophy	7	Lotus 30	–	Ford v8	1st	–	–
Mar 20	Saloon car	Silverstone	Saloon car race	61	Lotus Cortina	–	Ford T/C	–	–	–
Mar 26	Saloon car	Sebring	Three Hours Race	–	Lotus Cortina	–	Ford T/C	1st	–	–
Apr 4	F1/NC	Syracuse	Syracuse GP	18	Lotus 33	R11	Climax v8	1st	P	FL
Apr 10	F2	Snetterton	Autocar Trophy *Heat 1 2nd, heat 2 6th, overall 3rd*	12	Lotus 35	–	Cosworth SCA	3rd	–	–
Apr 10	Saloon car	Snetterton	Saloon car race *(in class)*	41	Lotus Cortina	–	Ford T/C	2nd	–	–
Apr 19	F1/NC	Goodwood	Sunday Mirror Trophy	5	25	R6	Climax v8	1st	–	FL
Apr 19	Sports car	Goodwood	Lavant Cup	33	Lotus 30	–	Ford v8	1st	–	–
Apr 19	Saloon car	Goodwood	St Mary's Trophy	–	Lotus Cortina	–	Ford T/C	1st	–	–
Apr 25	F2	Pau	Pau GP	4	Lotus 35	–	Cosworth SCA	1st	–	FL
May 1	Sports car	Oulton Park	Tourist Trophy *Heat 1 ret lap 62, Heat 2 ret (gearbox)*	4	Lotus 30	–	Ford v8	–	–	–
May 31	Indy 500	Indianapolis	Indianapolis 500 *Start 2nd*	82	Lotus		Ford 4-CAM	1st	–	–
Jun 5	Sports car	Mosport		–	Lotus 30	–	Ford v8	ret	–	–
Jun 7	F2	Crystal Palace	London Trophy *Heat 1 1st, heat 2 1st, overall 1st*	15	Lotus 32	–	Cosworth SCA	1st	–	FL
Jun 7	Saloon car	Crystal Palace	BRSCC race	–	Lotus Cortina	–	Ford T/C	2nd	–	–
Jun 13	F1/WC	Spa-Francorchamps	Belgian GP	17	Lotus 33	–	Climax v8	1st	–	FL
Jun 27	F1/WC	Clermont-Ferrand	French GP *Pole, led from start lap to end*	–	Lotus 25	–	Climax v8	1st	P	FL
Jul 3	F2	Rheims	Rheims GP	6	Lotus 35	–	Cosworth SCA	3rd	–	–
Jul 10	F1/WC	Silverstone	British GP *Pole, led from start lap to end*	5	Lotus 33	–	Climax v8	1st	P	–
Jul 11	F2	Rouen	Rouen GP	6	Lotus 35	–	Cosworth SCA	1st	–	–
Jul 18	F1/WC	Zandvoort	Dutch GP *Pole, led from start lap to end*	–	Lotus 33	–	Climax v8	1st	–	FL
Aug 1	F1/WC	Nürburgring	German GP *Pole, led from start lap to end*	–	Lotus 33	–	Climax v8	1st	P	FL
Aug 15	F1/NC	Enna–Pergusa	Mediterranean GP	12	Lotus 33	R6	Climax v8	2nd	P	FL
Aug 30	F2/3	Brands Hatch	British Eagle Trophy	60	Lotus 35	–	Cosworth SCA	1st	–	–
Aug 30	Sports car	Brands Hatch	Guards Trophy *Heat 1 8th, heat 2 ret (took Denis Jenkinson round in practice)*	8	Lotus 40	–	Climax v8	–	–	–
Aug 30	Saloon car	Brands Hatch	Ilford Films Trophy *excluded - outside assistance*	181	Lotus Cortina	–	Ford T/C	ret	–	–
Sep 12	F1/WC	Monza	Italian GP *Qualified 3rd, led from start*	–	Lotus 33	–	Climax v8	10th	P	FL
Sep 18	F2	Oulton Park	International Gold Cup	4	Lotus 35	–	Cosworth SCA	6th	–	–
Sep 18	Saloon car	Oulton Park	Gold Cup meeting	105	Lotus Cortina	–	Ford T/C	2nd	–	–
Sep 25	F2	Oulton Park		–	Lotus 35	–	Cosworth SCA	1st	–	–
Oct 3	F1/WC	Watkins Glen	United States GP *Lap 11, engine*	–	Lotus 33	–	Climax v8	ret	–	–
Oct 31		Riverside	Time-Mirror GP	–	Lotus 40	–	Climax v8	2nd	–	–
Oct 24	F1/WC	Mexico City	Mexican GP *Lap 8, engine*	–	Lotus 33	–	Climax v8	ret	P	–

1966 – 6th in world championship: 16 points; winner Jack Brabham: 42 points

DATE	FORMULA	LOCATION	EVENT	NO	TYPE	CHASSIS	ENGINE	PLACE	P	FL
Jan 8		Pukekohe	New Zealand GP	–	Lotus 39	–	–	ret	–	–
Jan 15		Levin	Gold Leaf Trophy	–	Lotus 39	–	–	2nd	–	–
Jan 22		Christchurch	Lady Wigram Trophy	–	Lotus 39	–	–	ret	–	–
Jan 29		Invercargill	Teretonga Trophy	–	Lotus 39	–	–	ret	–	–
Feb 13		Warwick Farm	Tasman Cup	–	Lotus 39	–	–	1st	–	–
Feb 20		Lakeside	Australian GP	1	Lotus 39	–	–	3rd	–	–
Feb 27		Sandown Park	Tasman Cup	–	Lotus 39	–	–	2nd	–	–
Mar 6		Longford	Tasman Cup	8	Lotus 39	–	–	7th	–	–
Apr 8	Saloon car	Snetterton	Scott-Brown Trophy meeting *(1st class)*	112	Lotus Cortina	–	Ford v8	3rd	–	–
Apr 11	F2	Goodwood	Sunday Mirror Trophy *Lap 12 – puncture*	1	Lotus 35	–	Cosworth SCA	ret	–	–
Apr 11	Saloon car	Goodwood	St Mary's Trophy *(1st class)*	91	Lotus Cortina	–	Ford T/C	4th	–	–
Apr 17	F2	Pau	Pau GP	2	Lotus 35	–	Cosworth SCA	7th	–	–
Apr 24	F2	Barcelona	Juan Jover *Engine failure*	1	Lotus 44	–	Cosworth SCA	ret	–	–
May 22	F1/WC	Monte Carlo	Monaco GP *Lap 60, suspension*	4	Lotus 33	–	Climax v8	ret	P	–
May 30	Indy 500	Indianapolis	Indianapolis 500 *Started 2nd. Led for 66 laps. Won by Graham Hill.*	19	Lotus	–	Ford 4-CAM	2nd	–	–
Jun 12	F1/WC	Spa-Francorchamps	Belgian GP *1st lap, accident*	10	Lotus 33	–	Climax v8	ret	–	–
Jul 3	F1/WC	Reims–Gueux	French GP *Did not start, hit by bird in qualification*	–	Lotus 33	–	Climax v8	–	–	–
Jul 16	F1/WC	Brands Hatch	British GP *Suffered from brake problems*	1	Lotus 33	–	Climax v8	4th	–	–
Jul 24	F1/WC	Zandvoort	Dutch GP *Water pump problems*	6	Lotus 33	–	Climax v8	3rd	–	–
Aug 7	F1/WC	Nürburgring	German GP *Lap 11, accident*	1	Lotus 33	–	Climax v8	ret	P	–
Aug 21	F2	Karlskoga	Swedish GP	3	Lotus 44	–	Cosworth SCA	3rd	–	–
Aug 28	F2	Keimola		–	Lotus 44	–	Cosworth SCA	3rd	–	–
Aug 29	Saloon car	Brands Hatch	Edward Lewis Shoes Trophy	215	Lotus Cortina	–	Ford T/C	1st	–	–
	Sports car	Brands Hatch	Guards Trophy *Heat 1 1st in class, heat 2 retired*	–	–	–	–	ret	–	–
Sep 4	F1/WC	Monza	Italian GP *58 laps, gearbox*	22	Lotus 43	–	B.R.M. H16	ret	–	–
Sep 11	F2	Montlhery	Montlhery GP	–	Lotus 44	–	Cosworth SCA	2nd	–	–
Sep 17	F1/NC	Oulton Park	International Gold Cup	2	Lotus 33	R14	Climax v8	3rd	–	–
Sep 17	Saloon car	Oulton Park		89	Lotus Cortina	–	Ford T/C	1st	–	–
Oct 2	F1/WC	Watkins Glen NY	United States GP	1	Lotus 43	–	B.R.M. H16	1st	–	–
Oct 23	F1/WC	Mexico City	Mexican GP *9 laps, gearbox*	1	Lotus 43	–	B.R.M. H16	ret	–	–
Oct 30	F2	Brands Hatch	Motor Show '200' *Heat 3rd, Final 3rd*	3	Lotus 44	–	Cosworth SCA	3rd	–	–
Oct 30	Saloon car	Brands Hatch	Lombank Trophy	5	Lotus Cortina	–	Ford T/C	1st	–	–
Nov 19	Rally	England	RAC Rally	8	Lotus Cortina	MK1	Ford T/C	ret	–	–

1967 – 3rd in world championship: 41 points; winner Denny Hulme: 51 points

DATE	FORMULA	LOCATION	EVENT	NO	TYPE	CHASSIS	ENGINE	PLACE	P	FL
Jan 2	F1/WC	Kyalami	South African GP *Lap 22, engine*	–	Lotus 43	–	B.R.M. H16	ret	–	–
Jan 7	F1	Pukekohe	New Zealand GP	–	Lotus 33	–	Climax v8	2nd	–	–
Jan 14	F1	Levin	Tasman Cup	–	Lotus 33	–	Climax v8	1st	–	–
Jan 21	F1	Christchurch	Lady Wigram Trophy	–	Lotus 33	–	Climax v8	1st	–	–
Jan 28	F1	Invercargill	Teretonga Trophy	–	Lotus 33	–	Climax v8	1st	–	–
Feb 12	F1	Lakeside	Tasman Cup	1	Lotus 33	–	Climax v8	1st	–	–

1967

DATE	FORMULA	LOCATION	EVENT	NO	TYPE	CHASSIS	ENGINE	PLACE	P	FL
Feb 19	FI	Warwick Farm	Australian GP	9	Lotus 33	–	Climax v8	2nd	–	–
Feb 26	FI	Sandown Park	Tasman Cup	–	Lotus 33	–	Climax v8	1st	–	–
Mar 6	FI	Longford	Tasman Cup	–	Lotus 33	–	Climax v8	2nd	–	–
Apr 2	F2	Pau	Pau GP	–	Lotus 48	–	Cosworth FVA	4th	P	FL
Apr 9	F2	Barcelona	Barcelona GP	–	Lotus 48	–	Cosworth FVA	1st	–	FL
Apr 23	F2	Nürburgring	Eifelrennen	–	Lotus 48	–	Cosworth FVA	ret	P	–
May 7	FI/WC	Monte Carlo	Monaco GP *Lap 42, suspension*	12	Lotus 33	–	Climax v8	ret	–	FL
May 21	F2	Zolder	Limbourg GP *Heat 1 1st, heat 2 4th, retired in final*	–	Lotus 48	–	Cosworth FVA	ret	–	FL
May 30	Indy 500	Indianapolis	Indianapolis 500 *Ret with piston problems after 35 laps*	31	Lotus-Ford 38/7	–	–	31st	–	–
Jun 4	GP	Zandvoort	Dutch GP *Qualified 8th, first race in the Lotus 49*	5	Lotus 49	–	Cosworth Ford v8	1st	–	FL
Jun 18	GP	Spa-Francorchamps	Belgian GP *Pole*	21	Lotus 49	–	Cosworth Ford v8	6th	P	–
Jun 25	F2	Rheims	Rheims GP	–	Lotus 48	–	Cosworth FVA	ret	–	–
Jul 2	FI/WC	Le Mans	French GP *Lap 23, transmission*	6	Lotus 49	–	Cosworth Ford v8	ret	–	–
Jul 9	F2	Rouen	Rouen-Les-Essarts GP	–	Lotus 48	–	Cosworth FVA	ret	–	–
Jul 15	FI/WC	Silverstone	British GP *Pole, last race in Britain*	5	Lotus 49	–	Cosworth Ford v8	1st	P	FL
Jul 16	F2	Tulln-Langenlebarn	Flugplatzrennen Tulln-Langenlebarn	–	Lotus 48	–	Cosworth FVA	ret	–	–
Jul 23	F2	Jarama	Madrid GP	–	Lotus 48	–	Cosworth FVA	1st	–	FL
Aug 13	F2	Karlskoga	Swedish GP	–	Lotus 48	–	Cosworth FVA	3rd	–	–
Aug 6	FI/WC	Nürburgring	German GP *Lap 4, suspension*	3	Lotus 49	–	Cosworth Ford v8	ret	P	–
Aug 27	FI/WC	Mosport Park	Canadian GP *Lap 69, ignition*	3	Lotus 49	–	Cosworth Ford v8	ret	P	FL
Sep 3	F2	Keimola	Finnish GP	–	Lotus 48	–	Cosworth FVA	1st	P	FL
Sep 5	F2	Hameenlina	Hameenlinnaloppet	–	Lotus 48	–	Cosworth FVA	3rd	P	–
Sept 10	FI/WC	Monza	Italian GP *Pole, lost race on last lap*	–	Lotus 49	–	Cosworth Ford v8	3rd	P	FL
Sep 24	F2	Albi	Albi GP	–	Lotus 48	–	Cosworth FVA	3rd	–	–
Oct 1	GP	Watkins Glen	United States GP	5	Lotus 49	–	Cosworth Ford v8	1st	–	–
Oct 22	FI/WC	Mexico City	Mexican GP *Pole*	5	Lotus 49	–	Cosworth Ford v8	1st	P	FL
Oct 29	Stock cars	Rockingham	Rockingham 500	–	Ford Fairline	–	–	ret	–	–
Nov 5	USAC	Riverside	Rex Mays 300	–	Vollstedt Ford	–	–	ret	–	–
Nov 12	FI/NC	Jarama	Spanish GP	1	Lotus 49	RI	Cosworth Ford v8	1st	P	F

1968 – *11th in world championship: 9 points; winner Graham Hill: 48 points*

DATE	FORMULA	LOCATION	EVENT	NO	TYPE	CHASSIS	ENGINE	PLACE	P	FL
Jan 1	GP	Kyalami	South African GP *Pole, last Grand Prix win*	4	Lotus 49	–	Cosworth Ford v8	1st–P		FL
Jan 6	FI	Pukekohe	New Zealand GP	–	Lotus 49	–	Cosworth Ford v8	ret	P	–
Jan 13	FI	Levin	Tasman Cup	–	Lotus 49	–	Cosworth Ford v8	ret	–	–
Jan 20	FI	Christchurch	Lady Wigram Trophy	–	Lotus 49	–	Cosworth Ford v8	1st	P	FL
Jan 28	FI	Invercargill	Teretonga	–	Lotus 49	–	Cosworth Ford v8	2nd	–	FL
Feb 11	FI	Surfer's Paradise	Tasman Cup	6	Lotus 49	–	Cosworth Ford v8	1st	–	–
Feb 18	FI	Warwick Farm	Tasman Cup	–	Lotus 49	–	Cosworth Ford v8	1st	P	–
Feb 25	FI	Sandown Park	Australian GP	–	Lotus 49	–	Cosworth Ford v8	1st	–	–
Mar 4	FI	Longford	Tasman Cup	–	Lotus 49	–	Cosworth Ford v8	5th	–	–
Mar 31	F2	Barcelona	Barcelona GP *Car badly smashed up*	–	Lotus 48	–	Cosworth FVA	ret	–	–
Apr 7	F2	Hockenheim	Deutschland Trophee *Crashed & killed in rebuilt car from Barcelona*	1	Lotus 48	RI	Cosworth FVA	DNF	–	–

A note on Race Statistics

Key:

FI/WC: A world championship Grand Prix

FI/NC: A non-championship Grand Prix

P: Pole position

FL: Fastest lap

These statistics have been compiled from various sources, many contradictory, and are not complete. The Jim Clark Room at Duns Museum would be happy to hear from anyone with corrections or missing information. Please email the curator, Andrew Tulloch, on a.tulloch@scotborders.gov.uk

Bibliography

Clark, Jim *Jim Clark at the Wheel* London: Arthur Barker, 1964

Darley Peter *Jim Clark: Life at Team Lotus* Luton & Littleton, Colorado: Coterie Press Ltd., 2007

Dymock, Eric *Jim Clark: Racing Legend* London: J.H. Haynes & Co. Ltd., 1997

Gauld, Graham *Jim Clark, Portrait of a Great Driver* London: Hamlyn, 1968

Gauld, Graham *Jim Clark Remembered* Wellingborough: Patrick Stephens Ltd., 1984

Gauld, Graham *Jim Clark, The Legend Lives On* Wellingborough: Patrick Stephens Ltd., 1994

Nye, Doug *Autocourse Driver Profile: Jim Clark* Richmond, Surrey, UK: Hazleton, 1991

Young, Eoin *Jim Clark and His Most Successful Lotus* London J.H. Haynes & Co. Ltd., 2004

The archives of *Motor Sport* magazine, www.motorsportmagazine.co.uk

Photographic sources

Index

First published in Great Britain in 2008
by Weidenfeld & Nicolson
10 9 8 7 6 5 4 3 2 1

A CIP catalogue record for this book is available from
the British Library.

ISBN: 978 0 297 85440 1

Design by Jean-Michel Dentand
Editorial by Suzanne Arnold

Printed and bound in Germany by Mohn media

Weidenfeld & Nicolson
The Orion Publishing Group Ltd
Orion House
5 Upper St Martin's Lane
London WC2H 9EA

An Hachette Livre UK Company

The Orion Publishing Group's policy is to use papers that are natural,
renewable and recyclable products and made from wood grown in
sustainable forests. The logging and manufacturing processes are
expected to conform to the environmental regulations of the country
of origin.